The New America

Also by Mark Little

Turn Left at Greenland
Zulu Time

The New America

Mark Little

NEW
ISLAND

The New America
First published 2008
by New Island
2 Brookside
Dundrum Road
Dublin 14

www.newisland.ie

ISBN 978-1-84840-012-2

British Library Cataloguing Data. A CIP catalogue record for this book is available
from the British Library.

Book design by Inka Hagen.
Typeset by TypeIT, Dublin.
Index by John Ryan
Printed and bound in the UK by CPI Mackays, Chatham ME5 8TD

10 9 8 7 6 5 4 3 2 1

Acknowledgments

I would like to offer my eternal gratitude to Tara Peterman for being my guiding light during the writing of this book, and apologise to Tommie, Daisy and Sorcha for my absences during the past year.

Once again, I owe a great debt to literary agent Jonathan Williams for his clarity and warmth. All at New Island have done a tremendous job in bringing this book to life, in particular Deirdre Nolan.

I would also like to acknowledge the guidance and support of my colleagues and editors at RTÉ during my travels through the 'New America', especially Ed Mulhall, Noel Curran and David Nally. Adrian Lynch of Animo Productions and Ruan Megan played a key role in developing some of the central themes of this book. They also taught me that there is a lot more to communicating big ideas than writing them down.

Friends and family have helped shape this book. In particular, I would like to thank Tom Little and Neil Leyden for offering game-changing advice at critical moments.

Mark Little
August 2008

Gatsby believed in the green light, the orgastic future that year by year recedes before us. It eluded us then, but that's no matter — tomorrow we will run faster, stretch our arms farther . . . And one fine morning — So we beat on, boats against the current, borne back ceaselessly into the past.

F. Scott Fitzgerald, *The Great Gatsby*

Contents

Introduction:
The Game

Scottsdale – Sunset in the Shining City

The towering columns of thundercloud circling the stadium are dark with the promise of rain but no one pays them much heed.

'That's one of the things you discover living here,' says the school official. 'The rainstorms never seem to make it beyond the edge of the city. Must be something to do with all that concrete and asphalt.'

The last storm of summer will send nothing more than a brisk warm breeze across the playing fields of Saguaro High School tonight. The opening game of the football season will kick off in front of a golden sunset. This is Scottsdale, Arizona. It could be no other way.

The Saguaro Sabercats are defending state champions. In tonight's game, the team will face the Prescott Badgers. Not the fiercest opposition they can expect this year. Truth be told, the biggest obstacles that the players will face this season are their own expectations. Here and now, in the late golden hour of a desert evening, what you hear through gritted teeth is the sound of young men straining to keep their demons in check.

The Sabercats are on the field now, with just over a half-hour to game time. They play in black and gold: boys in men's uniforms.

A coach in khaki pants and a white golf shirt directs a series of exercise routines. Three parallel lines of players are crouched down on the pitch as if profoundly constipated, their shiny black helmets on the ground beside them. They keep that position for what seems like an age, until a coach lets out a guttural grunt.

'Up.'

They rise, limber, unblocked. The coach shouts out a question which is audible only to a football player's ear.

'Dropmedownsareyoualright?'

The boys respond from the back of their throats.

'Igh.'

Then another instruction.

'Begin.'

The boys start their jumping jacks: arms and legs, out and in. But their gloved hands rise only to the level of their shoulders, so this abbreviated routine appears both impatient and slightly camp. With each cycle they chant:

> One, two, three, C,
> One, two, three, A,
> One, two, three, T,
> One, two, three, S,
> S ... S ... S

They are the Cats. This cycle is complete. The boys run out of formation with a long, manly wail ending in an emphatic, high-pitched war cry: 'OOOO-wwwww.'

There is much crying out and high-fiving, but there are also moments of solitude as players come to rest on the sidelines. One stands slightly aloof, his face obscured by his helmet, thinking deep thoughts behind layers of plastic and styrofoam. He is still breathless from the warm-up. His mouth hangs open as his chest rises and falls. Absentmindedly, he adjusts the metal grid on the front of the helmet as if looking for some karmic balance between heavily protected head and pounding heart. Then he is at rest. Static. Unsmiling. Pumped.

The loudspeakers pour out the bass-laden drone of death-metal and rap music, breaking the tranquillity of the evening, guarding the young men against the complacency of calm.

The boys of defence began to drift toward the sideline. A voice in the developing huddle barks: 'Bring it up.'

The Defensive Coach addresses his boys, now gathered around him in a tight circle of brawn and congested aggression.

'Lot of work. Spring. Summer. Lifting. Push-ups. Sit-ups. Lifting. Everything you worked for. Everything you worked for. This here's where the fun starts.'

He delivers the words in a monotone, stripped of emotion. The boys are like ravenous birds picking at a carcass. Glass-eyed. Determined.

'Got to be prepared. Mentally prepared and you will be fine.'

Sensing the pep talk has run its course, deep, young voices in the huddle trade snippets of inspirational gibberish:

'Let's go. We're in red and blue, we're in red and blue.'

'Stay in it. Let's go.'

'This is where the VO2s pay off.'

'Atta boy. Here we go. Watch the hop.'

It's over now. The boys of defence have one last ritual to observe. They come closer and clasp hands and call out a single word as they do:

'Intensity!'

Saguaro is the rule, not the exception. The lowliest American town will turn out on a Friday night to celebrate their juvenile heroes in playing fields with big stands seating many hundreds, if not thousands, of fans. Local TV crews are often there to record the action (as they are at Saguaro on opening night) and, at the very least, there is a commentator to call the plays on the PA system. The action will unfold against a backdrop of beautiful noise created by marching bands and cheerleaders.

High school football exists in a separate universe from the schoolboy leagues of an Irish childhood. The players will never know what it is like to outnumber a handful of dutiful parents shivering on a blustery sideline. They will never change hurriedly in a tin hut smelling of cowshit and Deep Heat. There's no chance that they will travel home from an away game, knee-to-muck-knee in the back of a borrowed Hiace van. We live our schoolboy dreams in stark, brutal prose. They preen themselves with epic, inflated poetry.

Mike Garcia is the coach responsible for all the equipment that the Sabercats will use tonight. To everyone at Saguaro, he is known as Tug. His big round face, framed by a neat goatee beard, is moist from the last rays of the fading sun.

'You really breathe this. Friday night. From a very young age. It's Friday night and there's thousands at a game. You live for a Friday night.'

Tug drives away with one leg hanging out the side of his golf cart, his eyes darting around in search of an unresolved detail.

The big stand framing the playing field is filling up with the home crowd. The track just in front is alive with the colour and sensual promise of cheerleaders. Their uniforms are black and gold, absorbing and reflecting the glow of the evening sun.

Five girls move clear of their friends to practise their human pyramid. One young woman is lifted skyward by the hands of others. She reaches maximum altitude with her right arm pushed into the sky at the very same angle as her left leg.

The pose is held for not more than a couple of seconds before the young woman on top begins to fall. As she goes from vertical to horizontal, her body executes a perfect twirl before her four friends catch her. She is at rest. Pristine. Controlled. Incorruptible.

It's getting near floodlight time as the cheerleaders finish their warm-up and assemble under one of the goalposts. Two of them hold a white paper banner wrapped around a giant hula-hoop, painted with the words 'Beat the Badgers'.

The marching band strikes up as the players run out in single file to the acclaim of the home crowd. They gather in the shade of the banner, scores of beefy young men trying to hide behind a wall of paper and cheerleaders. We can see them, we know what's coming, but what the hell.

The team crashes through the banner with the sound of bass drums, brass and human voices rising into the bruising sky. They run around for a while before settling on the sideline, facing the flag on a high, narrow flagpole. The band strikes up *The Star-Spangled Banner*.

The sun has left behind just enough light to illuminate an approaching blanket of twilight cloud. The Sabercats and their coaches look like they have already lived through hours of physical combat. Beads of sweat have gathered around the thick black marks smeared beneath the eyes of their biggest players.

The anthem is over. Heads disappear into helmets again. Sabercats are on the move. Time for one last huddle, one final burst of inspirational jargon only the boys will understand.

'Here we go, baby. Let's kick off.'

'You show me some kick-off, you show me some, boys.'

Sabercats win the toss.

The players dance through the early plays, skipping over the grass as if it were red-hot embers, moving their heads vertically and horizontally in momentary spasms. The ball disappears into a car-crash of colour. Gold and black for Saguaro, blue and white for Prescott. Number 46 emerges from the wreckage of bodies and pushes his fist into the warm air, jumping and twirling, swinging his hand as if he were slapping an imaginary backside. Sabercats have gained control of the game. They have taken one step closer to their destiny.

At an American football game, you are surrounded on all sides by agitation. Unrest spreads like a pandemic from band-members and cheerleaders to spectators, and from coaches to players. Even when there is a pause in the action, there are the frenetic gymnastics of the cheerleaders and the music, urging you to move. For God's sake, just move.

Perhaps because of that perpetual frenzy, American football

doesn't travel well. It has to be consumed on the spot, as a spectacle, wrapped up in a ribbon of beautiful noise, magnified by thousands of spectators watching young men being transformed into storybook heroes.

On Friday nights, in towns and suburbs across America, high school football does the impossible: it reminds people why a country with a manic devotion to the individual survives as a nation. Football offers reinvention, but also sanctuary.

Up in the stands, thousands of supporters have come together to worship the civic creed of football. One of them is Herman Serignese, who was principal of Saguaro High for ten years. He speaks gruffly, with an East coast accent, suggesting a life-story shaped by an immigrant experience of America. If not his, then his family's.

'I moved to Arizona thirty years ago to improve life for me and my kids and it's worked out great. You get up and work hard and do your best and things work out for you.'

'And you get to watch Friday night football, right?'

'You come to Friday night football coz it represents the whole American spirit. It embodies everything that America is about.'

Herman points to the field now. The Sabercats are rolling over Prescott and he is warming to his theme.

'They work hard and have a lot of pride and they have a lot of discipline.'

Pride is everywhere. Oozing from every pore. The type of pride that forgives all division and repels all doubt.

'People criticise, but I will be truthful … I don't really care what other people think about America.'

'After all the problems of the last eight years … ?'

'What problems … what problems we got? Sure, we had to deal with a terrorist attack and got involved in a war in Iraq but that's just the way it has been.'

In the eyes of a patriotic man like Herman, those calamities were like natural disasters, they come with the territory. When the aftershocks subside, this will still be the shining city.

'America is the greatest country in the world. No doubt about it in my mind. People fight to get in this country. Name me another country people fight to get into. People dying to get in this country. Literally dying.'

He gestures with both hands to the pitch and almost laughs, as if it would be ridiculous not to see this.

'You won't get me to change my mind. It's great. It's like being in heaven.'

—•—

Pride. Dynamism. Destiny. Words that enchant Americans at their moments of greatest opportunity and deepest difficulty.

When Herman Serignese told us that he was living in heaven, he was speaking for a majority of Americans. In virtually every global survey of happiness, Americans are more satisfied with their lives than people in almost any other nation. The great observer of early American life, Alexis de Tocqueville, put this optimism down to 'a lively faith in the perfectability of man'.

It has been that way ever since the Puritan preacher John Winthrop set the earliest American settlers a momentous challenge in 1630: 'For we must consider that we shall be as a city upon a hill. The eyes of all people are upon us.' Winthrop borrowed this image from the 'Sermon on the Mount', in which Jesus said: 'A city set on a hill cannot be hid.' Jesus compared that city to a lamp: 'Let your light so shine before men, that they may see your good works.' So was born the shining city, a vision of the earthly paradise America is destined to be.

Not everyone will end up at rest in their own personal Garden of Eden, but that's not the point. Belief in the American dream creates an actual pursuit of happiness. It may be inspired by a myth, but it is a noble myth which sparks movement on a breath-taking scale.

American history is the story of this transition from fairy tale to fact and it is a tale of contradictions and contrasts. The greatest contrast of all is between hope and fear. American optimism is nowhere near as absolute as the good people at Saguaro High lead you to believe. Hope is the engine of the American dream, but fear is the fuel.

What is often overlooked is the central role of failure in the American dream. To begin with, there is the doctrine of virtuous failure: when you chase big ambitions, it is accepted that you will stumble along the way. That kind of failure is simply proof that you are trying.

There also a greater existential fear that America will turn out to be an illusion. Americans have battled that profound doubt since the Puritans made landfall in the New World. Right after those inspiring lines about the 'city on the hill', John Winthrop cautioned that 'if we shall deal falsely with our God in this work we have undertaken … we shall shame the faces of many of God's worthy servants, and cause their prayers to be turned into curses upon us til we be consumed out of the good land whither we are a-going.' Don't say he didn't warn you.

Broken dreams are a constant theme in American history. Perhaps the most literate of the founding fathers, Benjamin Franklin, once warned his countrymen: 'He that lives on hope, dies farting.' (Some scholars claim that Franklin was the victim of an unfortunate misprint and the word should have read 'fasting'. Either way, you get the point.)

As US history unfolds, talk of failure takes on an altogether darker tone. 'Ah my country! In thee is the reasonable hope of mankind not fulfilled,' thundered Ralph Waldo Emerson.

American literature is bursting with stories of broken dreams. One of the most powerful themes in American writing is the poisonous effects of constant change, the simmering rage and anxiety beneath all that happiness and optimism.

Once more, football is powerful metaphor, captured beautifully in the story of 'Swede' Levov, the tragic hero of Philip Roth's *American Pastoral*. A former high school football and baseball star, his beautiful life is torn apart by the social upheaval of the 1960s, and the bitterness of those around him: 'It was as though while their lives were rich and full they were secretly sick of themselves and couldn't wait to dispose of their sanity and their health and all sense of proportion so as to get down to that other self, the true self, who was a wholly deluded fuckup.'

The battle between hope and fear feeds into a much broader American contradiction between the individual and the collective. On the face of it, the United States is nothing more than an enormous celebration of personal achievement. Look at American football, and the pedestal on which those star players are placed. Their prestige extends far beyond the playing field. They are masters of the high school universe. They are walking, talking reminders of the difference between individual failure and success.

The cult of the individual reminds every outsider, nerd and oddball that individual success comes in all shapes and sizes. One of the classic American tales is of a courageous misfit who emerges from the frontier and faces down the close-minded establishment. The modern classic is the story of the internet pioneer. In the words of Steve Wozniak, the man who co-designed the first Apple computer, 'All the ideas that mattered to me came from outsiders.'

The celebration of the individual explains the powerful grip of a free-market ideology on the American psyche. More so than people in any other Western nation, Americans are convinced that each person is responsible for his or her destiny. Among forty-four nations surveyed by the prestigious Pew Research Center, America believed most strongly that failure is about the individual and not about society.

Belief is one thing, but historical fact is another. Americans may think of themselves as a nation of individuals, but their way of life has been shaped by the collective. Take another look at our football team. The star player is the quarterback: the lonely, vulnerable hero who throws the winning pass into wide open spaces. But he would be pulverised were it not for the blocking tackles of others. He would be nothing without that vast back-room team.

It is one of the great unspoken realities of American life that the path to every individual's destiny is paved by a bureaucracy. Consider the explosion of migration that followed World War II: returning veterans who had fought for their country now demanded their own personal slice of the American dream. As the old song says, 'How you gonna keep 'em down on the farm after they've seen Paris.'

It was the federal government which allowed them to chase their dreams by expanding the highway network in the post-war years. Throughout the 1940s and 1950s, one in five Americans changed homes every year, taking to the road to perform what Jack Kerouac described as 'our one and noble function of the time, move'.

They could not have moved without team players like Sam Schoen, who founded U-Haul in 1945 and began hiring out distinctive orange and white trucks and trailers to migrating Americans. As one of Schoen's colleagues would later say: 'Ford built the cars. The Government built the roads. We built the trailers.'

Schoen liberated individual yearnings, but he preached the virtues of the organisation, summing up his business philosophy with the initials IFDOAS: Intelligently Follow the Directions of a Superior. Schoen believed in profit but also in national interest, telling workers that 'the United States allows us to exist and it would not long continue to do so if we did not put its interests first.' The 'group-think' of Sam Schoen is as much a part of the American story as the individualism of Steve Wozniak.

The rivalry of the individual and the collective, the clash of hope and doubt, have shaped American history with the same frenzied certainty that we witnessed at that football game. At first, it can be hard to see any logic in the spectacular collision of forces, but look closer and you begin to understand a method in the madness.

There are guiding rules and boundaries to the march of American history, and they were put in place during the nineteenth century as waves of pioneers headed west in search of their 'manifest destiny'. As they began to settle, America's contradictory impulses were subsumed into two rival forces: 'Frontier' and 'Ritual'.

Frontier is the spirit of individual pursuit. It embraces personal freedom, innovation, dissent, endurance, and self-reliance, but also isolation, insecurity, and ruthlessness.

Ritual is the spirit of the community. It involves cooperation, law, faith, patriotism, and civic pride, but also rules, conformity, and self-righteousness.

Think of Frontier and Ritual as two competing 'teams' battling for control of the American personality. A drift towards the worst aspect of one personality tends to provoke a rise in the best aspects of the other, but the effort to strike a balance is an uncertain, messy and often painful journey. This creative tension is the hidden code that unlocks America's past, present and future.

The first person to really capture the permanent dysfunction unleashed by America's westward expansion was Frederick Jackson Turner. In a landmark speech in 1893 he summed up the spirit of the frontier as 'that restless nervous energy, that dominant individualism working for good and evil, withal that buoyancy and exuberance which comes with freedom'. Turner believed that the great surge into the vast western wilderness made the US a coherent nation. It was on 'the crucible of the frontier [that] the immigrants were Americanised'.

Turner realised that the frontier was a place of disorder as well as dynamism. 'The frontier is productive of individualism,' Turner wrote. 'The tendency is anti-social. It produces antipathy to control, and particularly to any self-control.'

The spirit of Frontier would have to be contained if it was to survive. As the pioneers of frontier life became settlers, they needed order in their lives. They looked to shared rituals to make the frontier fit for human habitation. The first great ritual was justice; for every outlaw, there had to be a sheriff. As towns became communities, the rituals of faith and family life soon followed. For commerce to thrive, property had to be protected, land had to be divided, and the federal government had to set boundaries. As the frontiers expanded, the rituals of patriotism became even more important, providing the glue that held together a nation of almost uncontainable contradictions.

The creative tension of Ritual and Frontier has mattered most during America's periodic bouts of reinvention and trauma. The great transformational leaders of the past fifty years have tried to relieve the fear of change by invoking Ritual. Martin Luther King relied on explicit patriotism in that momentous speech in Washington in 1963: 'Land where my fathers died, land of the Pilgrims' pride. From every mountainside, let freedom ring!' When it suits them, politicians also stoke up fear by invoking images of the Frontier. Remember how George W. Bush chose to frame his 'war on terror' in the days after 9/11. 'I want justice,' he said. 'There's an old poster out West, as I recall, that said, "Wanted: Dead or Alive".'

When politicians are looking for a lesson in how to balance Ritual and Frontier, they look to Ronald Reagan, who came to power during America's post-Vietnam, post-Watergate crisis of confidence. Reagan understood that Americans were looking for more than a recognition of their insecurity. He offered to turn their fears into historical parable. He posed as the rugged individual of old, who would clean up the town and face down the outlaws. He walked with a swagger, but talked softly about the future with the accent of the past, as his biographer Lou Cannon would later put it.

Reagan had his own fantasy version of the shining city, and its cornerstones were Frontier and Ritual:

> I've spoken of the shining city all my political life, but I don't know if I ever quite communicated what I saw when I said it. But in my mind it was a tall proud city built on rocks stronger than oceans, wind-swept, God-blessed, and teeming with people of all kinds living in harmony and peace, a city with free ports that hummed with commerce and creativity, and if there had to be city walls, the walls had doors and the doors were open to anyone with the will and the heart to get here.

Ronald Reagan realised that at a turning point in history, Americans want clear contrasts to guide them, alternate images of Ritual and Frontier. With the help of the San Francisco advertising guru Hal Riney, Reagan offered that contrast during his successful bid for re-election in 1984. His 'bear in the woods' advert captures the Frontier side of the equation. Riney is the narrator. He speaks over the sound of a heartbeat and images of a big brown bear in the forest: 'There is a bear in the woods … Some people say the bear is tame. Others say it's vicious and dangerous.' In the final seconds, an anonymous man approaches the bear. 'Since no one can really be sure who is right, isn't it smart to be as strong as the bear … if there is a bear?' The advert told Americans they still lived on the frontier and all that stood between good and evil was a rugged individual.

The second commercial, 'Morning in America', is about the revival of Ritual. The music is rich and upbeat and every frame appears to have been filmed at sunrise. 'It's morning again in America,' says Riney. We then see images of a young couple at

15

their new home, a boy saluting the flag, and a mother attending her daughter's wedding. 'This afternoon 6,500 young men and women will be married, and with inflation at less than half of what it was just four years ago, they can look forward with confidence to the future.'

To many around the world, Reagan was defined by a dangerous, fearful foreign policy, but to plenty of Americans he delivered renewal. He found the combination of Ritual and Frontier which matched his turbulent moment in history. In doing so, he changed the way that politicians talk about the pain that comes with great change.

Reagan would have an impact on Democrats as well as Republicans. He taught them that transformational leaders need to connect with history, take account of doubt as well as hope, and speak to voters in language they do not normally associate with politics.

Reagan's brand of Frontier and Ritual still shapes American politics. It echoes through the rhetoric of the 2008 presidential election. John McCain and Barack Obama draw heavily from the past, from Reagan all the way back to Winthrop, as they search for language to match the hopes and fears of the new America.

—•—

The first great transformational force in the new America is the tension between individual optimism and collective gloom. In April 2008, a *New York Times*/CBS News opinion poll found that 81 per cent of people believed that 'things have pretty seriously gotten off on the wrong track,' up from 35 per cent in early 2002. Americans today are more pessimistic about government's ability to solve problems than they were in 1974 at the height of the Watergate scandal and the end of the Vietnam War.

For all that collective pessimism, Americans appear to be personally optimistic. A series of polls taken in 2007 found that an overwhelming majority were content with their job and their family income, and expected their personal circumstances to improve. In a poll taken by the Pew Research Center, 65 per cent of Americans said that they were satisfied overall with their lives, which is one of the highest rates of personal satisfaction in the world. This unprecedented gap between public gloom and private happiness poses a major challenge for politicians. Voters clearly want change in the way America is governed, but most are wary of change that will jeopardise their personal security. The winning candidate in 2008 will be the one who resolves this contradiction between personal optimism and collective doubt.

John McCain and Barack Obama both seem to understand the challenge they face. They both speak about doubt in a far more explicit way than most American politicians. McCain talks about doubt in the language of the 'silent generation' who came of age in the stifling Cold War certainties of the 1950s. More than most public figures, McCain has known darkness. While he chooses not dwell on the mental scars of his years of captivity in Vietnam, he gave a revealing speech in March 2008 in which he talked of the stark realities of his childhood.

> When I was five years old, a car pulled up in front of our house in New London, Connecticut, and a Navy officer rolled down the window, and shouted at my father that the Japanese had bombed Pearl Harbor. My father immediately left for the submarine base where he was stationed. I rarely saw him again for four years. My grandfather, who commanded the fast carrier task force under Admiral Halsey, came home from the war exhausted from the burdens he had borne, and died the next day.

By his own admission, John McCain confronted doubt by rebelling. He has spoken openly about his tantrums as a child

17

and his reckless behaviour on his return from Vietnam. But he emerged from the darkness with a fierce appreciation of his country, and its exalted sense of honour and ritual. At a moment of national soul-searching, that is a deeply attractive proposition.

Initially, it is hard to see any sign of doubt in Barack Obama. In front of every crowd, Obama is always one charming, languid gesture away from smug. But doubt was actually an essential part of Obama's appeal. He turned his battle with doubt into a parable about his generation, those raised in the shadow of Vietnam, Watergate and the oil crisis.

Obama talked about his relationship with the American dream as if it were a difficult parent. In his campaign book, *The Audacity of Hope*, he wrote that as a man of mixed heritage, he had 'no choice but to believe in a vision of America'. He spoke of love and affection for his elders, but also of alienation. In a groundbreaking speech on race in March 2008, he spoke about his grandmother, 'who on more than one occasion has uttered racial or ethnic stereotypes that made me cringe'. Most striking is the way he described his grandfather in his first book, *Dreams from My Father*.

> His was an American character, one typical of men of his generation, men who embraced the notion of freedom and individualism and the open road without knowing its price, and whose enthusiasms could as easily lead to the cowardice of McCarthyism as to the heroics of World War II. Men who were both dangerous and promising precisely because of a fundamental innocence; men prone, in the end, to disappointment.

These words express the wariness of the generations driving American reinvention. They still believe in destiny, still feel the thrill of restlessness, but they believe that the American dream will have to change if it is to survive. A new balance will have to be found between hope and doubt, between the individual and the collective.

Obama's solution is a blend of Ritual and Frontier best expressed in a speech he made after losing to Hillary Clinton in the New Hampshire primary in January 2008. 'We will remember that there is something happening in America,' he said that night, 'and together, we will begin the next great chapter in the American story with three words that will ring from coast to coast … from sea to shining sea … Yes. We. Can.'

The speech inspired a musician called Will-i-am to create a video that would become a viral sensation on YouTube. The singer used the words and images of Obama's speech and set it to a musical soundtrack performed by a group of hip actors, musicians and sportspeople. Reagan has his 'Morning in America' ad. Obama had the 'Yes We Can' video. By May 2008, it had been viewed more than eight million times.

'It was a creed written into the founding documents that declared the destiny of a nation, YES WE CAN.'

In any other election, you would expect Obama's Republican opponent to define himself in opposition to such collectivist sentiments. But it is remarkable the extent to which John McCain has laid claim to the spirit of that speech, with its celebration of tradition, destiny and civic purpose.

On the night in June 2008 when Obama claimed the Democratic nomination, McCain responded with a speech in which he promised a new era of cooperation in American politics:

> I have seen Republicans and Democrats achieve great things together. When the stakes were high and it mattered most, I've seen them work together in common purpose, as we did in the weeks after

September 11th. This kind of cooperation has made all the difference at crucial turns in our history. It has given us hope in difficult times. It has moved America forward. And that, my friends, is the kind of change we need right now.

The vital similarity between Obama and McCain is captured by that word – change. Both recognise that their nation is embarking on a period of transformation, no matter who wins the 2008 election. They both understand that something *is* happening in America.

'This is, indeed, a change election,' said McCain, in that speech in June. 'No matter who wins this election, the direction of this country is going to change dramatically.'

Just like Ronald Reagan, McCain and Obama are looking for a blend of Ritual and Frontier which matches a moment of transformation in American life. They share an emphasis on the value of cooperation rather than the primacy of the individual, but they have different approaches to the hopes and fears that are shaping the new America.

Obama is more closely aligned with the forces that are transforming American life; he urges Americans to embrace a new frontier and all and risk and potential that goes with it. McCain is better equipped to address the doubts that come with change; he offers to revive American rituals and sustain them in the face of the challenges ahead. It is around this contrast that the 2008 election will turn. Yet, above all else, there is one fundamental truth in this contest: the transformation of America will continue, no matter who becomes the next president of the United States.

Every American reinvention involves soaring rhetoric and bitter debate, but the real driving force is something far more substantial: the unstoppable movement of people. The new America will not be defined by any single politician; it will be shaped by the millions of immigrants due to arrive in America in the coming years, the millions of Americans who are about to come of age, and the millions who have already followed their destiny to a sun-kissed frontier, somewhere out west.

Part One: The Place

1.
Surprise – The Sunbelt Frontier

Some people say the frontier is a state of mind. They are wrong.

The frontier is a real place. It runs along the edge of the Arizona boomtown of Surprise. About a hundred yards beyond a bingo hall called the Riverboat Village, just before West Bell Road becomes Sun Valley Parkway, there is a sign which says, 'Next service 10 miles.' That's it. The frontier. The boundary of the shining city. The spot where the insatiable desires of a 'westering nation' collide with the savage certainty of the wilderness.

If you are not paying attention, the border will be passed by as a peripheral blur. But with your senses primed, you will feel the churning sensation of flight, as if you had just hurled yourself off the edge of the map. If you are lucky enough to realise that you have reached the frontier, it is worth pulling over to appreciate the savage certainty of the boundary which bisects Arizona's Sonoran desert.

Looking back, your eyes are drawn to the hazy outline of the Phoenix cityscape, a good twenty-five miles away. In the near distance is the pronounced edge of the low-slung city of Surprise, marked by a long line of houses in various stages of completion, their timber ribcages and stucco box frames sitting in mute testament to the thrusting human hand that created this frontier.

If you had continued driving away from the city, the highway would have led you on a meandering journey around the 30,000 acres of Arizona's largest mountain park. On either side of the road there is nothing but desert stretching across the steepening slopes of the White Tank Mountains. Every couple of miles, a yellow sign repeats the warning 'Watch for animals'. Coyotes, raccoons, squirrels, cactus wrens, roadrunners, rattlesnakes and the occasional wandering mountain lion rule the wilderness side of the frontier. Were it not for the sanctity of the mountain park, that frontier would have already been pushed farther into the desert, making way for the metropolitan beast that churns up an acre of land every hour.

Somewhere in the desert are inanimate reminders of human life in the form of petroglyphs carved into the occasional rock. These are the visual record of the world as seen by ancient Native American tribes like the Hohokam, who first settled the Valley of the Sun, in which Phoenix now sits. The drawings were etched into a substance known as 'desert varnish', a unique geological substance that forms on clay-covered rocks which have been baked and frozen by the wild fluctuations of day and night in the desert. Just a few years ago, a petroglyph etched into desert varnish was discovered in the White Tank Mountains which scientists believe could be the only record in the western hemisphere of a supernova that appeared in 1006, the brightest supernova visible from earth for more than 5,000 years.

The desert provided a canvas for the very earliest Americans to create a vision of reality that was both mundane and fantastical at the very same time. In the 21st century, their descendants had their own version of desert varnish in the endless expanse of light brown stucco and manicured greenery that now creeps across the desert.

—•—

When they were naming towns in Arizona, impulse seems to have played an important role. How else do you explain Snowflake, Bumble Bee, Friendly Corner, Happy Jack, Two Guns and the deliciously toxic Arsenic Tubs? The names of

Arizonan towns can also pose an existential challenge, as in Why, draw attention from an unfortunate past, as in Brilliant (formerly known as Swastika), or simply describe the first thing early settlers saw in the fields around them (which probably explains the towns of Cherry, Strawberry and Sunflower).

Occasionally the name tells a story of old frontier days, which is certainly the case in the eastern Arizona mountain resort of Show Low. Legend has it that two duelling neighbours named Cooley and Clark decided that the town wasn't big enough for both of them. They chose to play cards to decide who could stay. At a crucial moment, Clark told Cooley, 'If you can show low, you win'. Cooley drew a deuce of clubs. 'Show low it is', he said.

In each of these names you hear the sound of a restless nation. As Arizona's official state historian, Marshall Trimble, puts it: 'it was almost as if the people didn't expect to be there very long.'

Perhaps Homer C. Ludden had movement on his mind when he founded the city of Surprise in 1937, naming it after his home town in Nebraska. As a state legislator and property developer, he was an ambitious man, but there was no earthly reason to think his new creation would amount to anything; Surprise was nothing more than a single gas station and a few houses dropped onto a square mile of farmland. That is pretty much the way it would stay for more than half a century.

The turning point came in the 1990s when retirees flooded into the Phoenix area looking for a lease of life in the dry, clear air of the Sonora Desert. Surprise bordered one of the biggest new retirement communities in the Phoenix area, the Sun City Grand, and it wasn't long before it succumbed to the onward march of manicured country clubs, early-bird restaurants and 'age-restricted' housing developments. By 1995, 10,000 people lived in Surprise and during the next five years the population would more than triple.

After the surge of elders came a torrent of young, low-income families fleeing congested urban areas, particularly those in California. They may have had limited means but they brought unlimited potential, and by the end of the twentieth century Surprise was the fastest-growing city in what would soon be the fastest-growing state in the Union.

The 2006 census estimates put the population at 85,000, but in 2007 city officials claimed that more than 100,000 people lived in Surprise. The same officials say that their city has another three decades of growth in it and expect the population to reach 650,000 by 2040, which would be sixty-five times the number living there just a half century before. To put this in context, the 2000 census found that just 44 people still lived in Homer C. Ludden's hometown in Nebraska.

As you struggle to find words to describe Surprise, you could easily settle on exceptional, but that would be misleading. Surprise is an outpost on a new American frontier which winds its way from California's Inland Empire, through the Mojave and Sonora Deserts, across the Colorado River and the Rio Grande, bisecting border towns like Las Cruces and San Antonio, running through the Hill Country of Texas, and skirting around the vast urban black hole that is Dallas before reaching the Gulf of Mexico. On this boundary, the divinely mandated pursuit that has defined America since the Pilgrims stepped off their boats is creating countless boomtowns like Surprise.

This new frontier is the product of America's obsession with movement, and specifically a surge of migration which began in the 1990s, when 73 million Americans crossed state lines to set up a new home. By 2005, it was estimated that one in seven were moving house every single year. The traffic was almost all one way: Americans were making a decisive shift away from overcrowded cities in the North and East and heading towards an unprecedented urban experiment rising from the arid earth of the Southwest.

The historic scale of this modern gold-rush was revealed by the 2000 US census, which found that America's population centre is moving south and west at a rate of three feet per hour, five miles per year. In the past 40 years, 84 per cent of the growth in the US population has occurred in the south and west of the country, and the current predictions are that by 2030 two out of three Americans will live in what is commonly known as the Sunbelt. The closest anyone has come to finding a name for all this is the 'Great Dispersal', a phrase coined by author and commentator David Brooks.

This is not just a population shift but a change in the focal point of American life. One hundred years ago, all ten of the biggest cities in the US were within 500 miles of the Canadian border. Today, the Census Bureau reports that seven of the ten most populous cities are within 500 miles of Mexico. Phoenix has replaced the birthplace of American democracy, Philadelphia, as America's fifth-largest metropolitan area. In the words of America's most respected demographer, William Frey, 'It's hard to think of the cradle of liberty being overtaken by a rough-and-tumble Western town, but that tells you something about the nature of our country. We're a country that's always seeking new horizons.'

Phoenix is by no means the only magnetic force at work in this Great Dispersal. While Arizona was the fastest-growing state in the US in 2006, Nevada had held that title for the previous 19 years, and its biggest city, Las Vegas, saw its population increase by 250% in a quarter of a century. Parts of Texas have also become a draw for those seeking a new life, with the state capital, Austin, increasing in size by 140% in recent decades.

Not everyone fleeing the big coastal cities makes it as far as the desert; a constant stream of migrants continues to leave Los Angeles, but many of them get only as far as the boomtowns of Riverside and San Bernardino, which lie just beyond L.A. County. Cities like Surprise have been cropping up with increasing frequency in what is being called the 'New Sunbelt', which includes Georgia, Utah, Colorado and the Carolinas.

29

I want to keep our focus on the stretch of the 'Sunbelt Frontier' that fits within traditional boundaries of the West and Southwest, not just because that makes it easier to measure, but because the changes there have more clarity and potentially more consequence than others. The Great Dispersal as it affects California, Nevada, Arizona, New Mexico and Texas is an unprecedented collision of all the forces that have shaped the United States, in both recent years and recent centuries. It is as if this vast stretch of desert has become the country's particle accelerator, propelling the American dream towards a chain reaction with a million contradictory fragments of the past and present.

History burrows deeper into the collective psyche here, the birthplace of Wild West fable, and so does geography; the forces of the frontier take on a wild kinetic energy in a region shaped by a territorial boundary with Latin America. Perhaps most intriguing of all is the sweet-and-sour relationship between the citizens of the Southwest and the spacious but unforgiving environment they have chosen to live in; nothing illustrates the clash of dreams and reality that is America better than the search for paradise in a landscape that is as hot as hell.

Above all else, the Southwest seems to have liberated Americans from the accepted limits of city and suburb. Under endless skies, they live inside a vast, overlapping patchwork of sovereign neighbourhoods separated by variations of the same sun-kissed American dream.

—•—

Just as demographers try to gauge the width and breadth of the shift toward the Southwest, they are struggling to find a name for the way Americans choose to live once they have settled there. The word 'suburb' has long been irrelevant in analysing exploding cities like Surprise, but what do you put in its place?

'Exurb' caught on for a while, but it doesn't come close to describing the metropolitan experiment playing out in the American Southwest. Just how, for example, do you categorise the Phoenix suburb of Mesa, which is now bigger than Miami, Minneapolis, Cleveland or Atlanta? How do you label communities of 300,000 or 400,000 people in places which were unknown desert hamlets twenty years ago? As one demographer put it, the new exurban form of living is 'the dark matter of the universe': it's very hard to see, but somehow it has more mass than all the planets, stars and moons put together.

At one recent count, there were more than 50 words to describe the rise of sprawling new communities in the outer orbits of big American cities, particularly in the South and West. When you see some of the labels on that list –'galactic city', 'exopolis', 'edge city', 'penturbia' and 'urban galaxy' – you get the impression that Americans in their millions have moved to some futuristic colony on another planet. The analysis of these new metropolitan centres is infected by the same fear of the unknown which gripped ancient map-makers who imagined serpents at the edge of the known world.

The label that seems to fit the reality best is 'boomburb', coined by Professor Robert E. Lang of Virginia Tech. Strictly defined, it describes a city of more than 100,000 people in the shadow of a bigger city which has grown by double digits over a sustained period (the fairly predictable label for a booming exurb of between 50,000 and 100,000 people is 'baby boomburb'). So if you believe the claims of local officials, Surprise is now a boomburb of Phoenix. Again, we need to put that in context: there are seven other boomburbs in the greater Phoenix area, and all are bigger than Surprise.

If we broaden our view, we see that the Sunbelt has become a giant Petri dish for these evolving urban organisms. As of late 2007, there were 54 boomburbs in the United States, all but nine located in the Southwest. The fastest-growing among them is

Henderson, the runaway offspring of Las Vegas, which grew by more than 4,700 per cent in the last half of the 20th century. All along the Sunbelt Frontier, boomburbs are becoming forces to be reckoned with. You may not know much about Chandler, Mesquite, Arlington, Plano, or Tempe, but you could argue that they reveal more about the inner workings of the 'indispensable nation' than Los Angeles, New York or Washington.

The first important lesson about the boomburbs is that they have largely broken free of the gravitational pull of their once-dominant neighbour. For example, Surprise is no longer a satellite of Phoenix; it is an independent entity which has gone looking for its own balance of Frontier and Ritual in the footsteps of the earliest pioneers and settlers.

Boomburbs are cities in the US sense, and don't easily match the European definition. In American parlance, the word 'city' does not necessarily relate to the size of a community; plenty of cities in the US are nothing more than small towns. Instead, it is a political term indicating that a community is 'incorporated' and pretty much runs its own affairs.

Boomburbs are just such incorporated cities: fiercely independent entities in their own right, with considerable autonomy over their finances. But to build a tax base, they need to attract people from other places, and land from the private sector. So from the moment it is incorporated, the aspiring boomburb has an innate desire to expand, a sort of 'growth gene'.

It works like this: a property developer buys land on which he or she will build a housing development. The developer asks the city to annex the land and provide the basic amenities. In return, the city gets more tax revenue when new residents move in (it will often privatise essential services into the hands of residents, as we'll see later). If the developer also builds a shopping mall, the city can then expect more revenue from sales taxes. It may get extra land from the federal government and occasionally annex small unincorporated suburbs. The bigger it gets, the wider its tax base. At some point in this process, the satellite city becomes a boomburb.

What makes the Sunbelt Frontier so boomburb-friendly is that it is one of the few regions with the land to accommodate these new urban empires. Throughout American history, it was the West which provided the land that fed American expansion. In his timeless essay on the American frontier, Frederick Jackson Turner wrote: 'The Western wilds, from the Alleghenies to the Pacific, constituted the richest free gift that was ever spread out before civilised man.' He was correct, although he had less luck with his next prediction: 'Never again can such an opportunity come to the sons of men.' More than a century later, developers and planners keep building on the gift of free-ish land and –crucially – Americans keep flocking to the frontier to live on it.

—•—

They come in search of their destiny and their dream home, which are one and the same. Throughout American history, home-ownership has been the most enduring landmark of success. 'A man is not a whole and complete man,' said Walt Whitman, 'unless he owns a house and the ground it stands on.' The search for completeness led the original pioneers to log cabins and picket fences. Today, it pushes them all the way to that line in the sand in the Arizona desert.

The frontier runs for miles on either side of West Bell Road through a series of housing developments that offer every property in every conceivable colour and material, as long as it is brown stucco. The great observer of the infant United States, Alexis de Tocqueville, said that an American will build a house and sell it before the roof is on, and that is exactly what they are doing in the Carrington section of the Surprise Farms estate, on the boundary between civilisation and wilderness. There are cars in the driveways and kids cycling around the culs-de-sac, but some of the houses at the edge of the development are still unfinished, their timber frames exposed to the dry, scorching heat.

There are no straight lines in Surprise Farms. The early suburban planners introduced curved streets in the belief that they discouraged strangers from cruising the pristine new neighbourhoods they were creating. Today, they are still being used to persuade Americans that a suburban street offers sanctuary from the harsh geometry of city life.

The development is built facing inwards, so what you see from the main road are the ugly backsides of the houses, but follow the winding laneways into the development and each property takes a distinct personality. When you purchase a house here, you acquire a little design quirk so that you still feel like an individual. It could be a nuance, like an extra high portico, or more of a statement, like an extra thousand square feet of property.

The top price for a house in Carrington is $229,950 (€147,000 at the time of writing). That buys you four bedrooms, a two-car garage and two and a half bathrooms (and no, I don't know what half a bathroom looks like). Carrington sits right on the border between Surprise and the White Tank Mountain Park, which seems to make it marginally less expensive than houses deeper inside this evolving boomburb. From the look of the families in the development, this will be the first step on the property ladder for many of them, the first giant leap toward completeness.

The mania that infected Surprise and boomburbs like it at the very peak of its expansion has eased. Back in 2005, when they were building one new house every six minutes in Arizona, housing developments in Surprise had a lottery system for prospective buyers. Where there was no lottery to whittle down the crowds, people camped out overnight. Construction slowed and prices fell towards the end of 2007 as the wider sub-prime crisis hit investors all across America, but new residents are still coming and among the neat sub-divisions of this Sunbelt boomtown their dollar can still carry them much closer to their dreams.

If and when the young pioneers decide to move deeper into the heart of Surprise, they will have a stunning array of options, at least by comparison to a first- or second-time buyer in Ireland. As of the autumn of 2007, the average price of a house in Dublin was €411,000, which worked out at roughly $570,000. If you used that money to buy property in Surprise, your options would have included a five-bedroom house on West Becker Lane in the Rancho Gabriela subdivision with three bathrooms and more than 3,500 square feet of space: all that for $20,000 less than the price of the average house in Dublin.

On North 179th Drive there was a 3,000-square-foot house with four bedrooms and three bathrooms and space for four cars in the garage. The house was built in 2006 and had a private swimming pool. The only drawback is that it had no fireplace, which frankly, is not the deal-breaker it might have been back in Ireland.

Among the other houses you could have bought for the average price in Dublin, one extended to 4,366 square feet, while none were less than 3,000 square feet of living space. The average size of a house in Dublin in 2005 was 1,064 square feet.

Space to build a new life is what has drawn millions of Americans to the Sunbelt. Even now, after more than a decade of rapid development, there are a little over a thousand people living in every square kilometre of Phoenix, which compares favourably to Manhattan where the same space would be occupied by 25 times that number of people.

Surprise offers the completeness of ownership and space to breathe, but the magnetic X-factor is the promise of reinvention. The Sunbelt Frontier offers you the chance to be a pioneer and build your own personal version of the shining city. If you didn't get there in time to help to build your neighbourhood, you can

35

still vaguely smell the paint from the lustrous walls of your dream home. In late 2007, on houses.com, only one of the houses advertised for sale in Surprise was built before 1969; 506 were built between 2000 and 2005.

Space, reinvention and ownership. And constant sunshine. What's not to like about life in a boomburb? Well, perhaps the answer is that it is still a 'burb'. No matter how intense, spacious and sunny it may be, this is still the suburban experience, and is contaminated by decades of derision and cliché.

Look at how awful the American suburb looks to the average Hollywood director. Perhaps the most powerful indictment of the perceived emptiness and alienation of suburban life was *American Beauty*, in which Kevin Spacey plays a doomed suburban father who lives a brief moment of glorious rebellion before he is killed. The movie opens with this damning premonition: 'My name is Lester Burnham. This is my neighborhood; this is my street; this is my life. I am 42 years old; in less than a year I will be dead. Of course I don't know that yet, and, in a way, I am dead already.'

The conventional Hollywood wisdom about suburbanites is that they lack any self-awareness. When a rebellious spirit like Lester Burnham reminds them of their shallowness, they set out to destroy him. One of the chief suspects in his eventual murder is his viciously conformist spouse. 'That's my wife, Carolyn,' says Lester, by way of introduction. 'See the way the handle on her pruning shears matches her gardening clogs? That's not an accident.'

Such classy jabs at suburbia to make us feel lucky we do not live there. They remind us why we are better than suburbanites. Suburbia is the ultimate American morality tale; its emptiness makes our live so much fuller and rounded by comparison.

The reason those images feel so credible to us is that there always seemed to be evidence to back them up. To begin with, suburbs in the United States have traditionally lacked diversity.

They have been sanctuaries for the white middle class, fleeing the insecurity of multi-ethnic cities. Once there, these bourgeois refugees tend to gravitate towards people exactly like them, live in houses just like theirs and pursue their neighbourhoods' single transferable lifestyle.

The pressure to conform may be intense but, strangely, it does not seem to forge a genuine sense of community. The conventional wisdom suggests that the level of social engagement in the suburbs is far below what it is in the traditional city neighbourhood. Surveys have shown that this is especially true of young suburbanites, who have tended to participate less in their local government or politics.

An army of sociologists have come forward with credible theories to explain the apparent emptiness of suburban life. There are the obvious sources of alienation, such as the sheer sprawling scale of suburbia and the reliance on driving rather than walking. In the most insightful history of the American suburb, *Crabgrass Frontier*, Kenneth Jackson writes: 'Streets are no longer places to promenade and to meet, but passageways for high-powered machines'.

When neighbours become drivers, they lose any notion of kinship; they become competitors. The consequences are vividly illustrated in the book *Suburban Nation*, written by three reform-minded planners. 'You are competing for asphalt,' the authors say, 'and if you so much as hesitate or make a wrong move, your neighbour punishes you. … The social contract is voided.'

The book cites two studies to illustrate the effects of this alienation. First, a survey which showed that the highest percentage of road rage incidents were recorded in suburban counties (three of them Sunbelt boomburbs). The second was a psychological assesment for driver behaviour in car parks. It found that drivers took 21 per cent longer to leave a parking space if someone else was waiting for it, and 33 per cent longer if that person honked their horn.

The emergence of suburbs in the scorching Southwest also fostered the spread of another obstacle to social engagement: air-conditioning. It gave you yet another excuse to stay inside your dream home and avoid outside contact. Some blame air-conditioning for the death of the front porch, which acted as a kind of social magnet in traditional urban neighbourhoods. Neighbours would gather in the cool of the porch to talk and to bond.

Kenneth Jackson describes the front porch as the physical expression of community, 'where doors need not be locked, where everyone was like family, and where the iceman would forever make deliveries. With a front porch, one could live in Brigadoon, Shangri-La, and Camelot, all in one.'

Suburbia's latest incarnation, the boomburb, has been lumbered with the same old negative preconceptions. You hear the familiar disdain in that long list of labels for boomburbs. Some, like 'anti-city', 'stealth city', 'disurb' and 'slurb', present these new communities as urban vampires sucking the life out of decent, old-fashioned cities. You get a similar impression from the term 'exit ramp economy', which describes the extent to which these new centres leech their commercial life off the freeway network.

Somehow, we have become prisoners of our prejudices. In reality, the suburbs were never as empty as they were made out to be. Much of the case against against suburbia is based on studies from the 1950s and '60s and owes a lot more to anecdotal opinion than to established fact. But times change, and our perspectives need to change with them. It is time to say our final goodbye to Lester Burnham. May he rest in peace.

—•—

Life in the American suburb is being reshaped by a dramatic shift in preferences. There is a backlash against the privatisation ethic of old suburbia. In the boomburbs of the Southwest this rebellion is being expressed as a nostalgia for 'small-town values' and an elemental craving for community. This generation of settlers are desperately searching for a whole new set of civic bonds which have the potential fundamentally to reorder suburban life. This renewal of community spirit will be the cornerstone of a new civic era in American history.

You could see this process an another historic shift from the individual to the collective, but I prefer to view it through the prism of Frontier and Ritual. The rise of the boomburb is yet another rush to the frontier. The Americans now flocking to the South and West are pursuing the same dream that animated the original Wild West Pioneers. Now, as then, they discover that the frontier is harsh and unforgiving. The pioneer eventually becomes a settler who seeks to transform a collection of rugged individuals into a ordered community. The construction of that community will require the components of Ritual. They will provide the civic cement to transform the American frontier into the American heartland.

The bland conformism we associate with suburban life is being replaced by something more unpredictable, more rounded. The boomburb is an innovation in the way communities are built and, like every great innovation, it is going to have consequences far beyond its narrow borders. Frontier has collided with Ritual in the boomburbs of America and we might all feel the resulting tremors in the years to come.

In towns like Surprise, the brash individualism of the pioneer is clearly giving way to the civic rituals of the settler. Granted, you would be hard pressed to find evidence of reinvention as you drive into Surprise. Turning from Grand Avenue on to West Bell, there is nothing but all the usual franchises and generic commercial clutter. All that distinguishes Surprise from every other exurban thoroughfare in America is the classy desert foliage along the margins and the occasional citrus tree.

Driving seems to be the only sanctioned form of movement, so the visitor feels like a voyeur. As you cruise past the master-planned communities and private golf clubs along West Bell, you are a gatecrasher who can't find the house with the party. There are some nice new restaurants sprouting up along Bell, but something strange happens when you pull into the car park around the back. There is nothing behind the long line of stores and chain restaurants but an expanse of desert scrub. It feels like you have just wandered out back on a movie set and discovered, as Gertrude Stein once said of her Californian home town, 'there is no there there'.

But take a second look at your surroundings. What looks to an outsider like the heart of the boomburb is often the periphery of the lives of the people who live there. Home Depot, Subway, Target, Wal-Mart and Taco Bell are landmarks rather than a reflection of the lives people lead.

On your way into Surprise, you probably missed the signposts directing you to a hidden reality. At Greenway and Grand you saw the beautiful young woman speeding across the level crossing on a Harley, her long blonde hair blowing behind her. But did she register? There was the sprawling U-Haul centre at the corner of Bell and Grand but what did that tell you? You were probably too busy to notice the Sprouts wholefood market. And what about the Latino family with the big SUV that just passed you in the car park? Or the two teenage Goths flying by on skateboards? Or that giant baseball stadium you could see in the distance? Or the pathways around the artificial lake in the gated community you just passed? And what do they mean on those posters in the middle of the road, the ones that read, 'Surprise – Live, Work, Play'?

Let's take that last clue first. From the moment you arrive in Surprise, you feel the messianic spirit of civic reinvention. City officials have set out to transform what was once a rough frontier outpost into a 'perfect' community which satisfies that renewed desire for small-town life. The city's official website says: 'Surprise is a collection of distinctive neighbourhoods with a small town feel and big city amenities,' and it has done a remarkable job in selling itself as a kind of desert playground.

It successfully courted two of America's biggest baseball teams to set up their training camps in the city, luring them away from their old Florida bases, with the help of a $48 million training facility and stadium. That opened right about the same time as a regional library, aquatic centre, recreation centre and 57-acre public park – the centrepiece of a newly-created down-town, just like small towns used to have.

Surprise works on several levels, not all of them visible to the outsider. Like almost all boomburbs, it has the money to provide top-notch physical amenities such as schools, fire stations and hospitals, but to also satisfy the intangible desires for security, exclusivity and innovation. Each boomburb styles itself as a brand, selling potential residents a way of life that will distinguish them ever-so-subtly from the boomburb up the road.

Within the brands, there are sub-brands, like Prasada, a vast new master-planned community in Surprise which eventually will stretch over 3,300 acres. The name comes from the Sanskrit word for 'grace', which captures perfectly the sense of other-worldly contentment which fortifies these master-planned desert communities like fluoride in tap-water. Just to make completely sure that you know you are not in Kansas any more, the Prasada website greets you with a quote from Eleanor Roosevelt: 'The future belongs to those who believe in the beauty of their dreams.'

The word you hear over and over again in these boomburbs is 'lifestyle', as in the sales pitch for Prasada, which promises 'a dynamic community designed to stimulate the senses with architecture, activities and lifestyle pursuits.' Words like 'stimulate' and 'pursuit' matter deeply here. All across the Sunbelt Frontier, I imagine planners and developers trawling

41

through the thesaurus to find ways of summoning up an epic journey away from all the suburban clichés. The Prasada pitch speaks of walking and talking and communing with nature:

> Masterfully planned streetscapes, trail systems, family-oriented communities and open spaces will provide residents and visitors with a sense of renewal, and the project's unique architectural design will be carried throughout all aspects of the development, reflecting the fluid and refreshing nature of water. Reflecting the community-oriented nature of the development, Prasada's streetscapes and pedestrian facilities will be designed to provide easy navigation and encourage interaction.

Like any one of the mass-luxury brands which emerged from the last part of the 20th century, the boomburbs trade heavily on a shift in perception, promising intimacy amid the sprawl. Their planners are selling the very opposite of the calcified ethos which had become associated with the suburbs. While their new hyper-suburban experience shuns both the blandness of the old suburbs and the vulgarity of crumbling cities, it worships the notion of community.

Beyond the conformity of the strip mall are pathways, outdoor seating, bike paths, recreational lakes, soccer schools, self-help seminars, organic food stores, mega-churches and ethnic restaurants. Just like the fusion cuisine that has come to dominate American menus, the boomburb offers a blend of lifestyle trends that looks awkward but feels so 'tomorrow'. Boomburbs are, to quote Robert Lang, 'proving grounds for a 21st-century suburban cosmopolitanism'.

You would never describe the last generation of suburbs as 'hot', but that is exactly the label being sought and applied to many of the fastest-growing urban centres on the Sunbelt

Frontier. *Money* magazine looked at 271 small to mid-sized cities in the US to determine which were the hottest: in other words, the fast-growing cities where residents can 'expect big-time benefits from small-town life'. The boomburbs and baby boomburbs dominated the list and most of the hot towns were in the west, including the top three: Plano, Texas; Anaheim, California; and the Phoenix boomburb of Scottsdale.

The core of the Great Dispersal is a generation of young, upwardly mobile families who have given up on the coastal cities but not on their metropolitan ethos. Their shared aspiration is to create lasting, material change on the new frontier.

Generally, what these new pioneers are creating are communities with more depth and more potential than the suburbs that are firmly fixed in our minds. But it would be wrong to create an alternative but equally false generalisation. Not everyone in Surprise is a wine-sipping, world-travelling, bicycle-riding, granola-eating, new-age Liberal. This is still America. It is God's country.

And yet God is working in mysterious ways on the Sunbelt Frontier.

2.
Radiant – The Freestyle Evangelical

They look like the best wedding band you have ever seen. The older of the two female singers bounces on the soles of her feet in a way that makes you want to bounce with her. The woman sharing the melody with her has movie-star blonde locks and a pair of snazzy glasses on her pretty face. The young man beside her is playing acoustic guitar and leans into the microphone to add his voice, closing his eyes briefly and waving his long, curly black hair gently in time with the music. The second male voice belongs to a black singer wearing a fetching orange shirt. The bass player behind him catches the eye of his drummer and smiles. He has a red beard, a big earring and hair stiffened with gel.

Life doesn't get better than this. Playing music, spreading joy and singing the praises of the Lord God Almighty.

> The heavens declare your greatness,
> The oceans cry out to you,
> The mountains they bow down to you.
> So I join with the earth and give my faith to you.

Christian rock is an acquired taste but the band at Surprise's Radiant Church this Sunday morning makes it easy to like. The crowd streaming in the door of the cavernous auditorium wastes no time in showing its appreciation. The band has only been on stage for one song and there is already clapping and singing, with all ages following the lyrics streaming across two giant screens behind the band.

> Open the eyes of my heart – I want to see you.
> High and lifted up, shining in your glory.

This crowd makes no concession to formality. There is not a jacket or tie to be seen. In fact, you could count on one hand the number of people with long trousers and long-sleeved shirts. They have come to praise the Lord Jesus in shorts, T-shirts and assorted items of sporting apparel.

This doesn't mean that the swelling crowd lacks passion. Far from it, there is real devotion here. Some of the women have their hands in front of their faces, palms facing inwards. The young couple among them stand mute, their arms draped around each other, rocking gently but emphatically to the music.

Walking among them is a man in a red-print Hawaiian shirt. He bears himself well and is perhaps a little more subdued than the shirt suggests. His manner is authoritative but solicitous, like a hard-working hotel manager. Out of nowhere comes an occasional bearhug, arms wrapped around chests, palms pounding on backs (slightly less pounding with the ladies). This is Pastor Lee McFarland, founder of Radiant Church. Fisher of souls. God's brand manager in Surprise.

The band is now on its third song and Pastor McFarland is heading for the stage to join them.

> You are high and exalted, worthy of praise,
> With my heart I will love and adore.

The congregation senses that the service is about to begin and they hurry into the soft red, comfortable chairs arranged in gentle semi-circular rows facing the stage. There is not a pew,

45

statue, collection box or vestment in sight. This feels more like a cineplex cinema just before the lights go down and the show begins.

'Praise the Lord. God is amazing.'

Pastor Lee is merely thinking out loud on the stage. The official welcome is left to a very good-looking woman called Victoria, who appears in a taped message on the screens behind the stage.

'Please turn off your cellphones and put your pagers to vibrate.'

Then the main feature begins. Pastor Lee is sitting on a high stool behind a lectern and the first thing he is going to do is sell you a ticket to a water-park. There will be baptism in the warm waters of the wave pool at 9 a.m. this coming Saturday, followed by a day of food, fun and friendship.

'Now I know what you're thinking: "There is no way I want anyone from this church to see me in a bathing suit." You would be amazed when we go to Waterworld, God strikes us with a special kind of blindness. We can't see cellulite, we can't see wrinkles, we can't even see flesh.'

There is a drawl in the Pastor's voice: a slow, affected Southern touch. It makes him less preachy and gives his comedy shtick an authenticity it might not otherwise have.

'It looks like it's probably going to be hot.'

Irony from the preacher-man. The faithful laugh.

'It's a great way to spend a day as a family. It doesn't dawn on you until you are there about an hour and you start going: "This is cool."'

He draws the last three words out with the knowing tone of a hip teenager.

'You are saying, "Na, I don't want to get baptised; I'm going to get wet." Well, you are already wearing your swimsuit.'

After his sales pitch for the wave-pool baptism, Pastor Lee has a little more housekeeping to do (changing the date of the father-son camping trip) before he moves on. Then you think he is about to get serious. But the band strikes up again.

> God is bringing a brand new day.
> No more fear, it's a new day,
> no more worry, it's a new day.

And a couple of minutes later, the Pastor is back in his chair. This is it. Now he's going to rain some righteousness down upon us.

'Innit hot out there?'

Excuse me?

'It's so hot that chickens are laying hard-boiled eggs. It's so hot, the trees are whistling for the dog to come over.'

That hot, huh.

'It's so hot that if the temperature drops below 95 at night, you call it … ' – here the Pastor pauses and raises the middle two fingers of his hands in 'air-quotes'– 'chilly'.

Just one more time: how hot did you say it was?

'It's so hot, you get condensation on your butt from the hot water in the toilet bowl. That's really weird.'

Yes. He did say it. In a church. In front of a congregation of American evangelical Christians, an assembly not known for their love of anatomical gags or irony.

The Pastor went on too long for this to be simply a badly judged warm-up. The jokes got appreciative laughs in all the right places. Clearly, the faithful come to Radiant in the full expectation of an irreverent tone. The humour may be slightly off-colour, but it is gentle and inclusive. Pastor Lee knows his audience likes to be challenged but never judged, to be drawn out of themselves without ever leaving their comfort zones. Rather than lecture to them, his sermon is a running dialogue in which he plays their role and his own simultaneously. He is one of them, only better.

'Turn to Second Chronicles in your Bibles,' he tell the worshippers, signalling the approach of the sermon.

'The eyes of the Lord strengthen those who are fully committed to Him. If you are discouraged and a little tired and a little burnt out, this verse will become one of your life verses.'

The pastor can't seem to resist another joke.

'It's a bit like a breakfast of bacon and eggs. The chicken is involved but the pig is totally committed.'

Now comes the challenging part. The Pastor asks his audience what they are committed to during the various stages of their lives, from cradle to grave. What follows is less a spiritual pep-talk than a lesson in life, delivered in a mesmerising 30-second soundbite.

'Human nature does not want to serve other people. Human nature says "let's talk about me". Who is going to meet my needs? People will leave a marriage saying: my needs are not being met. People will have an affair: my needs are not being met. Who is going to help me? Who is going to take care of me? Who is going to give to me what's due to me? Me, me, me, me, me.'

All the lost souls in their T-shirts and shorts are bonded at that moment. They are no longer alone with their human weakness; it has been shared and diluted and ultimately will be erased, as long as they heed Pastor Lee and his gentle call for collective redemption.

'And Jesus says you gotta lose that. You gotta lose that. Give up that type of focus in order to find true life. God says stop worrying about your own welfare and start helping out.'

And Radiant is where you start helping out. The very act of turning up today is the first step to salvation. Pastor Lee is waiting to make you feel special, loved, appreciated.

'Do you know what's made Radiant Church such an amazing church? *You* are amazing. You are the secret of Radiant Church. Hundreds of you volunteer here each weekend. We still need you. You are amazing. When you come forward and say "I want to be involved", we say "We've been waiting for you." '

If the medium is the message, then Radiant speaks volumes. It tells you more about the evolution of suburban life in America now than any mocking Hollywood movie or dry, academic treatise. In Radiant, we see the move from Frontier to Ritual unfolding before us in technicolour. In Pastor Lee McFarland we are presented with an American classic: the pioneer-turned-settler around whom history turns.

—•—

Back in 1996, he was simply Lee McFarland: a well-paid executive with Microsoft. He was an unsettled 36-year-old in search of a mission. He loved God and had enrolled in a correspondence course to teach him how to be an evangelical pastor. But what happened next was far beyond the call of religious duty.

McFarland quit his job, sold his house, packed up his SUV and drove with his wife and two kids from Washington state to Surprise, then a lonely, desert hamlet (and, as McFarland would later recall 'a radically unchurched area'). He set out to recruit members for a new church, but the initial response was disappointing. He soon tried a more informal approach, going from door to door in the new housing developments in T-shirt and jeans asking questions about what these new, young families wanted from religion. He took the answers, came up with the sales pitch for Radiant Church, and put it in a leaflet posted through the letterboxes of thousands of those light-brown stucco houses: 'At Radiant you'll hear a rockin' band and a positive, relevant message. Come as you are. We won't beg for your money. Your kids will love it!'

Pastor Lee held his first service in the hall of a local elementary school in September 1997 and 150 people turned up.

Within two years, the attendance was 350, which the new preacher thought was a perfect size for an informal and intimate church. But he had not reckoned on the wild expansion of Surprise or the lure of Radiant's laid-back Christianity. By 2002, Pastor Lee was preaching to a weekly congregation of 2,000 people, which made Radiant officially a 'mega-church'. The congregation would eventually swell to 5,000 and force Radiant to build a new campus to accommodate the crowds and the stunning array of innovations which define the church.

Pastor Lee's formal 'sermon' is just one part of the Radiant experience. When it is over, the real business begins. You leave the main auditorium through a set of wide double doors into a lobby filled with desert sun, streaming through the high glass ceilings. To your left is a long trestle table laden down with a mound of Dunkin' Donuts and an orderly queue forming in front of it.

Since every Sunday is a perfect Sunday at Radiant, there is good coffee to go with your doughnut. The Radiant Café dominates the far corner of the lobby, with its brown marble counter and giant chalk-board menu hanging over the heads of its young volunteer staff. Before you order, a young woman behind the counter asks you for your first name.

'Hi, Mark, what can I get you?'

When the drink is served ('Triple-skinny-grande-latte for Mark') it comes in a Starbucks cup, which answers the question: what would Jesus drink? If he didn't have time to queue, he could always swing his car around to the Drive-Thru Latte stand in the parking lot.

The Radiant gift shop is just a few feet from the café and it is jam-packed with polite people in casual clothes. The shop sells any product that can carry an inspirational slogan or the word of God, from CDs to jewellery. The head sales assistant flits between racks of sweatshirts and T-shirts, answering questions and gauging sizes. She has jet-black hair interrupted by pronounced blonde streaks and is set apart from the shoppers by the stylishness of her clothes. She hardly has the time to tell you just how busy the shop has become. 'It's insane,' she says. 'We are begging for more room.'

The doughnuts and Starbucks and religious fashion arranged around that lobby form a first impression designed to tell the new arrivals that they are being offered a brand with hidden depths. When Pastor Lee talks about the marketing strategy at work in that lobby, he sounds every bit the former Microsoft salesman.

'We get them in the door by talking about things that are relevant to their lives. We might mail out a flyer that says: "How to have a great marriage. Come join us this summer and we'll talk about improving your marriage." Well, every married couple that reads that will think, "Maybe my marriage isn't the greatest." Then they'll go, "It's free, I'll get a doughnut. Wow, they have a Starbucks and they say it only lasts an hour. That's good. It doesn't encroach on my life." And then we say, "They are in the door. Now we can say more to them than just the marriage part."'

The trick works just as well on kids as it does on adults. Down the corridors which lead away from the lobby are a series of rooms devoted to Radiant's children's ministry. Mikki Garland used to be the children's pastor before she got promoted. She is bright, beautiful and down with the kids, but not so much that she couldn't pull off the occasional stern lecture. She's happy to provide a guided tour, knowing she will meet some familiar young faces, and when the first door is opened, a surge of noise and light floods out.

This is the 'Elevate' room, catering to children between the ages of 10 and 12. The energy in the room could light up a small city. There is a small stage where the host is gamely trying to keep the kids focussed on a competition that is actually a cover for what Pastor Mikki describes as an 'age-appropriate' Bible lesson. Radiant's kids band, Corn Dog Blue, are standing by, waiting for a chance to grab some attention in a room that is almost unbearably hyperactive.

There are games systems and televisions hanging down from the ceiling, pool tables and basketball hoops in the corner and a set of round couches they call 'the conversation pit', although it is hard to see how anybody, let alone a pre-pubescent child, could concentrate on the spoken word when everywhere they look is another stimulus. The kids rush backwards and forwards in front of the stage like crashing waves on a sunny shore. One or two stop briefly to high-five Mikki. A young girl gives her a hug. As she untangles herself, Mikki describes the method to this madness.

'We asked these kids: what do you want to see when you walk in the church? What's your dream? They said we want basketball and games systems and live music. So we made it happen. We gotta keep them coming back week after week.'

'And they come back with their parents?'

'Right.'

'And that's the idea?'

'That's right.'

Mikki is smiling now, happy to see that the broader game plan is appreciated.

'We are winning. We are succeeding.'

Nobody here feels the slightest bit embarrassed that they have turned God into a mega-brand. Another church might resent the observation that its main building looks like a shopping mall. At Radiant, that is a selling-point. Another preacher might object when a magazine writer describes Radiant as 'the blue jeans church'. Pastor Lee posts the comment on his website.

'Marketing the church is sometimes felt to be a bad thing,' the Pastor says. 'But Jesus was the ultimate marketer. He said, "I will make you fishers of men." These days he might have said, "I will make you a great marketing manager."'

It would be easy to equate the hard sell at Radiant with the money-grabbing TV evangelists of the 1980s, the kind who sold hellfire and damnation and lived in mansions. But that would be a mistake. There is no evidence that Pastor Lee does this to enrich himself. Apart from his prized Harley-Davidson, he shows no outward sign of wealth. In fact, I detect a wistfulness in his daughter's voice when she describes the life of luxury her family left behind when the pastor left Microsoft.

The monied televangelists of the 1980s are what American Christianity used to be. Radiant is what it has become: a fierce free market in which churches must become distinct brands to preserve market share. The mega-church has the same economies of scale as a corporation, giving it the ability to provide a far more comprehensive 'lifestyle experience' than the local branch of the big religious franchises, whether they are Catholic or Protestant. A church like Radiant is always looking for an unseen niche, and that requires careful, almost obsessive, attention to the detail of daily life. That makes a church like Radiant an unerringly accurate barometer of the tastes of its catchment area, in this case the boomburb of Surprise.

Competition has always defined the American religious experience. Many countries have an established religion linked directly to the institutions of the state. In the United States, church and state are officially separated. You would think that would weaken religion by removing it from the public sphere, but the opposite is the case. Religion has had the freedom to develop independently of government into a great marketplace of ideas and beliefs. Each church competes for congregations and each Christian is encouraged to act like a consumer, testing out variations of their favourite brand. The latest surveys shows that 40 per cent of Americans have changed their religious affiliation since childhood, making the market for God a particularly volatile one.

It is becoming ever more volatile thanks to the Great

Dispersal. As millions of Americans move to the Sunbelt, they leave behind their old churches and go looking for new ones. Increasingly, they search for a new form of religious experience, one that reflects the contours of their new lifestyle. Religion must change to suit their lives and not the other way around. The new generation of pioneers are looking for their own personal Jesus.

The United States is still among the most religious societies in the western world with 70 per cent of Americans saying religion is important to their lives. But a growing number (14 per cent) declare that it is not, reflecting a small but significant secular shift in US society. There is also an increasing proportion of Americans who describe themselves as 'spiritual' or 'religious' but are disenchanted with the established religious denominations. One in six Americans now say they have no fixed affiliation to any church and that rises to one in four among 18- to 29-year-olds.

These trends pose a challenge for the mega-churches, but they also create an opportunity. Houses of worship like Radiant must compete harder in a more individualised marketplace, but they are also better equipped to do so than smaller conventional churches. That advantage is reflected in their explosive growth; it is now thought that there are more than 1,000 evangelical churches in the United States with congregations of more than 2,000 people each. Mega-churches have grown fastest on the shifting sands of the Sunbelt Frontier and, while they each proclaim themselves to be unique, they are cut from exactly the same cloth. Pastor Lee likes to describe Radiant as 'the red-haired step-child' of the mainstream evangelical movement, but in truth there is a rapidly expanding brood of red-haired step-children who look set to inherit the family silver.

America's most successful churches follow the same corporate strategy as Radiant. Over at the Carson Valley Christian Centre in Nevada, Pastor John Jackson describes himself as a 'PastorPreneur' and has written a book with the same title. Other Boomburb mega-churches trade on a stunning array of services, from banking to tax advice. In Phoenix, the First Assembly of God has a store of medical equipment it lends to worshippers. In Houston, the Lakewood Church offers martial arts to what it calls 'Christian warriors', while across town the Second Baptist Church has a full-sized football field.

Far and away the biggest influence on the mega-church movement is Rick Warren, the founder of the Saddleback Church in California's Orange County. He is the original of the species. He sports a goatee beard and Hawaiian shirt and wears no socks. He fills his services with self-help advice and Christian rock, and he is the most successful religious entrepreneur on the planet. His book, *The Purpose-Driven Life*, has sold more than 25 million copies, putting it in the same league as *The Da Vinci Code*.

Warren has built up a model mega-church ministry at Saddleback, which attracts more than 20,000 people to its 120-acre campus every week. Such is the success of Warren's 'purpose-driven formula' that it has been adopted by tens of thousands of like-minded pastors. He compares his method to an Intel operating chip that can be inserted into the hard drive of any church.

Among Rick Warren's devoted followers is Pastor Lee McFarland, who learned much of what he knows about running a church during training conferences at Saddleback. When asked who is the person he most admires, Pastor Lee says Rick Warren.

We can see how the rise of the 'purpose-driven movement' is transforming the style of American religion, but is it changing the political outlook of the 40 per cent of Americans who describe themselves as evangelical? Churches like Radiant reflect the evolving preferences of the Sunbelt Frontier, but to what extent are they agents of transformation in American society? In short, is there any chance that the casual shirts and risqué humour represent a shift away from the fundamentalism we have come to associate with American Christianity?

The truth is that it is too early to tell.

Pastors like Lee McFarland and Rick Warren still deliver an uncompromising version of biblical reality amid all the talk of self-help and personal empowerment. Warren makes no secret of his belief that 'heaven and hell are real places' and that 'Jesus is coming again'.

The traditional theology of the mega-church is matched by a strong bias towards the Republican Party. Back in 2004, the demographic group that played the biggest role in George Bush's re-election was white evangelicals. Exit polls showed that Bush captured 78 per cent of their votes, a 10 per cent improvement on his performance in 2000.

So far, there is no evidence that the 'purpose-driven' movement has made American Christians dramatically more liberal. However, it has transformed the relationship between religion and politics in a substantial way, and that has everything to do with the evolving sensibilities of the Sunbelt boomburbs.

The movement, moderation and optimism which define a city like Surprise is giving rise to the 'Freestyle Evangelical'. The phrase is used to describe the new generation of Christian pastors who are moving beyond the narrow grounds of sex and morality to define their world view. These leaders are generally much younger than the traditionalists who have guided the evangelical movement, and they express a subtle disdain for the 'culture war' that has raged around profoundly divisive issues like homosexuality and abortion: so-called 'wedge' issues. The Freestyle Evangelical looks beyond the traditional boundaries of evangelical culture for new alliances, new issues and new influences. That's what makes the rising generation of boomburb pastors agents for change.

There are overt liberals within the purpose-driven movement,

like Joel Hunter, who runs a successful churc[...]
Florida resort city of Orlando. He is the author o[...]
*Wrong Bird: Why the Tactics of the Religious Right Won't F[...]
Conservative Christians*, a title that pretty much sells itself.[...]
the left of most traditional Christians but he was chosen [...] [...]
evangelical movement to be the voice of their campaign against
global warming called 'Creation Care'. Environmentalism is
increasingly a high priority for a younger generation of church
leaders who agree with Joel Hunter when he says, 'As Christians,
our faith in Jesus Christ compels us to love our neighbours and
to be stewards of God's creation.'

Evangelicals have not abandoned old certainties, but they
have broadened the agenda of Christian activism to include
issues where they have common ground with old liberal enemies.
So in those mega-churches you hear plenty of talk about Darfur,
climate change, social justice and volunteerism. You will also see
Freestyle Evangelicals building broader coalitions across partisan
and ideological lines.

Once again, Rick Warren has pointed the way forward,
creating alliances with the likes of Bono and Bill Gates in his
campaign for global justice, and courting controversy with his
campaign against HIV/AIDS. His decision to invite Barack
Obama to Saddleback Church for a conference on that issue in
2006 incensed traditional evangelicals. Warren was unrepentant
as he stood on the stage with Obama and conservative Senator
Sam Brownback. 'I've got two friends here, a Republican and a
Democrat,' Warren said. 'Why? Because you've got to have two
wings to fly.'

The leadership of pastors like Joel Hunter and Rick Warren
represent a gradual trend among Christians, not a radical break.
The Pew Foundation on Religion and Public Life has broken
down the evangelical community into traditionalists and
centrists. Its surveys suggest that the two camps are of about
equal size now, but experts agree that the centrist camp is

.wing. It may be a long-term process, but those Sunbelt mega-churches are already having a moderating influence on the relationship between religion and politics.

It is easy to misread the political sympathies of American Christians, particularly in light of George Bush's strong showing among evangelicals in 2004. Historically, American Christians have actually had political divided loyalties. A little over half of all evangelicals voted for Jimmy Carter back in 1976, and as many as one in three white evangelicals voted for Bill Clinton in 1996.

Successive Democratic candidates, including Barack Obama, have made great play of their faith. Back in 2000, George Bush was asked for his favourite philosopher. He famously said Jesus Christ. What few people remember is that his opponent, Al Gore, said that his guiding principle was 'What Would Jesus Do?'

The Freestyle Evangelicals have broader horizons, and while that does not necessarily mean they will turn Democrat overnight, it does mean they are part of the broader reinvention of American life. The boomburb mega-churches are mediators between Christianity and popular culture. Traditionalists sought to define their faith by what it was against. Pastors like Rick Warren and Lee McFarland judge success by their ability to prosper in the mainstream of American life. In this sense, they are agents of change. They know their markets. They understand that their Sunbelt congregations are chasing a version of the American dream that is both optimistic and personal. They know this latest generation of pioneers is looking for a form of religion that is confident, non-judgemental and adaptable.

Young Americans are still chasing individual dreams, but the mega-churches deliver the collective purpose they so clearly crave. The Freestyle Evangelical has come of age in a chaotic, bitter and harsh era. What they want most is sanctuary. They have had their fill of Frontier. Now it is time for Ritual.

—•—

Back in Surprise, the adult service is over, but the teenagers are still pumping with sweat and adrenaline on the south side of the Radiant campus. They are part of a weekly event called 'Octane', which is a tailored version of the Radiant formula: rock music, T-shirts and shorts and a sense of purpose.

The music is self-consciously edgy and the volume just short of deafening. The star of the church's youth band is an Asian-American bass-guitar player with a long dyed blond mop of hair cascading over his eyes. He plays with one foot resting on top of a speaker and his head rocking back and forth, inciting the teenager worshippers to move. A line of boys at various stages of adolescence responds by wrapping arms around each other and headbanging in time with the bass tones bouncing off the walls.

The student pastor, Travis Hearn, takes the stage during a break in the music to offer the teenagers a mission.

'Everyone stay standing. We are going to look for an offering to help our missions in the eastern Horn of Africa. Give generously. If you can spare your last $100 bill, it will all go to a water project.'

The pastor knows that there are not too many $100 bills in this crowd; he is being ironic. He speaks with Radiant's trademark irreverence, leading these young people to a cause greater than themselves, but never pushing them beyond their comfort zones. You also see something you were only partly aware of: a desperate attempt to reach a rising generation.

In everything we have seen in Radiant, the common denominator is youth. Those Hawaiian shirts and shorts and risqué jokes are not just part of a sales pitch; they are visible challenge to the mistakes of an older generations of Christian leaders.

'We are going to do an offering song. This song rocks. This is hot. This is your chance to go crazy. But first let's bow your heads. You guys can rock out after I offer a prayer.'

In another church the prayer might be drawn from a written

text, but here it comes in the loose, shifting syntax of a Freestyle Evangelical.

'God accept our offering. Use it for your kingdom. Use it for our friends in Africa, to offer them clean water and not just clean water, but living water – and that is you, Jesus.'

In the space of just two hours on the Radiant campus, you will be offered self-help, redemption, a crèche for the kids, a doughnut and coffee, and now a chance to save the world. If you decide to linger there is the promise of so much more. Come back on Friday night for 'Celebrate Recovery', a forum for the drug-addled, sex-addicted, chemically dependent, or generally messed-up individual in need of a psychological group hug. 'We all got stuff,' is the group's motto. 'Join us as we work on it together.'

Mikki Garland's recent promotion put her in charge of Radiant's counselling programmes. She seems a bit young to be shouldering such an intense burden, but under that layer of innocent warmth and good humour there is a steely, dispassionate core. As we walk back to the church's main building, she talks about some of the tragic cases she has taken on in recent months. She is counselling a young woman who is four months' pregnant and recently widowed. Her husband was killed when he wrapped his car around a tree. The first place she turned to was Radiant Church.

'I sometimes pinch myself,' she says, 'and ask why God has chosen me for such important work.'

Pastor Mikki started out at Radiant as an intern for Pastor Lee and then went to a Christian university in Texas where she met the man she describes as her 'soulmate'. Surprise drew her back, and now she and her husband both work at Radiant. As we walk through the lobby one last time, it becomes clear that Mikki is working through her own personal demons.

'When I was about five years old, my parents got a divorce and I just grew up thinking "I want to help people who are going through the same thing."'

Radiant is that kind of place. It invites you to reveal your hopes and your doubts and promises no judgement. All it asks of the people who walk through its doors is that they commit on some level to talking, sharing and taking part. It offers sanctuary, but also reinvention – that perfect balance between Frontier and Ritual.

The stragglers are still nursing their coffees and polishing off the doughnuts and Pastor Lee is walking among them, connecting.

'I've come maybe six or seven times,' says a plump young man who has brought his wife and two young sons. 'It's awesome.'

Pastor Lee nods and smiles, but instead of responding to the man, he turns to face the children.

'These are the boys, right?', he says, and points to one of the kids' T-shirt which carries the logo of a football team from Pittsburgh.

'Steelers? Oh my God. I'm a Broncos fan.'

Now it's clear why it is hard to accept Lee McFarland as a preacher. Radiant is a self-contained town and Pastor Lee is the Mayor. In his presence, in his church, with all these people around, you never have to worry about the troubles of the world. Here in the lobby of Radiant Church, between the doughnuts and the iced coffee, we have found the heart of a boomburb, the urban core we couldn't find as we drove up and down West Bell Road.

Radiant is an imperfect and partial example of transformation. After all, this particular town centre has its own restrictions. Just as those gated-communities exclude the 'other', the mega-church excludes the unbeliever. There will even be some faithful Christians who will see dangerous delusion and self-centredness in its rituals. Yet for all that, few places can guide us through the transition from Frontier to Ritual quite like Radiant. Not many people can explain the process of reinvention quite like Lee McFarland.

'Americans loves to reinvent themselves. They always want to start over and make it better. Our church is an example. You can drive five miles from here and you are in the middle of the desert. There is just something about creating a new community in the wilderness, one that is better than what we have left in the cities.'

Reinvention cannot happen without rebellion, but in the United States it's often hard to distinguish between the old order and the new. Sometimes all you have to go on are the coffee and doughnuts and the words of a computer salesman turned preacher.

'We challenged everything about church. We left no stone unturned. We just kept saying to ourselves, "Let's do it all different."'

3.
Gilbert – Conservative with a Small 'C'

Dave Rodriguez is a firefighter the same way other people are short or tall, blonde or red-haired: it's in his genes. His father was a volunteer member of the Fire Department, and as a kid Dave would follow him out on calls, cycling his bike in hot pursuit of the fire truck.

Dave grew up to become a battalion chief in the Fire Department in his hometown of Gilbert, Arizona, the fastest-growing city in the United States. A constant smile lights up his dark complexion, telling you that he can't quite believe he is being paid to do the very thing that makes him happiest.

Dave is the boss at the city's newest firehouse, which he also helped to design. He walks out of the gleaming, open-plan kitchen and dining area into a weight room that would do a big-city gym proud. Upstairs, there are individual bedrooms for his firefighters which look cleaner and more comfortable than you would expect from a mid-range hotel. But the feature that Dave is most proud of are the two brass poles at either end of the firehouse.

'I made sure the poles were mounted in front of a full-length window,' he explains, 'so that the kids going by might see a real firefighter in action.'

This is the fourth new firehouse built by the Gilbert Fire Department in just four years. Two more are under construction.

On this windy stretch of East Williams Field Road, the firehouse is one of the few buildings that is actually finished or not for sale. It is the anchor that will eventually secure the half-built community growing up around it.

Dave Rodriguez remembers what Gilbert looked like when it was just another hard-scrabble farming community. His grandfather settled here in the 1920s, when it was known as 'the hay capital of the world'. In 1970, 1,900 people lived in Gilbert. By 2007, the population was 191,000 and 1,000 new residents were coming every month. That's the equivalent of one new person arriving every hour of every day.

Gilbert certainly has that boomburb 'growth gene' but it also has a piece of civic DNA, an innate desire to renew community life. You hear when you listen to the city's mayor, Steve Berman, who says that Gilbert's eventual goal is 'to be the only 300,000-person small town in America.'

At a Labor Day barbecue, Dave Rodriguez gathers his newly assembled team and their families. Many are new arrivals who have come from out-of-state. Some traded workaday careers for one of the most venerated jobs in America. Almost every man in that firehouse repeats a variation of the same line to describe the complete fulfilment their jobs delivered: 'The only other job that could possibly be better than this is being a golfer on the PGA tour.'

Dave Green is perhaps the most striking of all. He talks of public service with the kind of unthinking innocence that confounds foreigners. He beat every other new recruit on the entrance exam for the Gilbert Fire Department, even though he is in his fifties. His wife is a police officer in a tough part of Phoenix. His son just left on his first deployment with the US Air Force to Iraq: 'Saying goodbye was the most difficult thing I have ever done in my life,' he says, his voice catching in his throat. Dave moved to the Sunbelt to work a little, play golf a lot and prepare for a comfortable retirement, but I suspect that he will not give up this job lightly. It sets him apart in a society where distinction is so hard to come by.

For others, a firefighter's job offers sanctuary from the dysfunction and disorder of life on the frontier. Jeff is the sunny, shaven-head driver of the newest truck in the firehouse, a job he loves almost as much as his hobby. 'Bro,' he says, with endearing intimacy, 'the only reason I'd give this up is if I had a shot at music.' Jeff then begins to talk in unsettling detail about his childhood travels with his father, who once played with the heavy-metal band, Stallion. The band had a measure of success in the 1970s when it toured with some of the rock legends of the day, including The Eagles and Kiss. As a boy, Jeff spent a lot of time on the road with his father and the band. The vice, addiction and excess around him taught Jeff all he needed to know about human frailty.

The boy became a man who loves three things above all: the shiny fire truck with the Stars and Stripes sprayed on the grille, his wife (whom he calls 'stud') and God (the word 'Yahweh' is tattooed on his arm in Hebrew lettering). Short of headlining a rock festival, life doesn't get better than this. Especially when you know how empty life can actually be.

Self-esteem gushes forth in conversation with Jeff and Dave Green, drawn from a bottomless well of community pride. Up there with faith and family, fighting fires is about the purest expression of the American ideal. It was that way before 9/11, but the sacrifices that the New York Fire Department made that day have cemented the status of the firefighter as the last remaining icon of the American frontier. In a desert boomburb like Gilbert, the firefighter is the modern Marlboro Man, an uber-masculine symbol of safety standing rock-solid in the midst of a deluge that threatens to wash away everything.

That firehouse in Gilbert brings Frontier and Ritual into perfect alignment. It stands as a sentinel amid the frenzied construction work continuing for miles along either side of East

Williams Field Road. It adds material and spiritual value to the community that is growing up around it. The boomburb brand promises small-town values, and that firehouse delivers them.

The new building has enough staff and equipment to cope with the Apocalypse, even though there will never be enough fires to justify the expense. It's best to think of this as a downpayment on the mental health of a frontier community. It is an expensive but effective way of telling a fresh generation of pioneers parking their U-Haul trucks and over-loaded SUVs in the driveways of their new Mission-style McMansions: the journey is over; you are home.

There is something touching about the huge investment of humanity and decency that has gone into these fire stations. To see the fastest-growing city in the United States guided by such genuine civic purpose gives you hope for America. In fact, it is tempting to see those firefighters as symbols of a new era, in which community replaces confrontation as the driving force in US politics.

Gilbert offers us that hope. But it also shows us how much would have to change.

—•—

It would be nice to leave Gilbert with one single image: a passing kid staring in awe at the heroic firefighter rushing to save a life. Unfortunately, that is not going to happen.

A few miles from the firehouse, we have just pulled up at a sandwich shop at the edge of a shopping complex on Val Vista Drive. Two police cars have crept into the car park and pulled up short of a dark blue SUV, just a hundred yards from where we are standing. Police officers emerge from their cars with pistols, drawn chest-high, pointing in the direction of a black man climbing out of the passenger door of the vehicle. They wait for him to clamber face down on to the scorched asphalt and put his hands behind his head before they approach, with pistols still drawn.

As more police cars arrived, there is the whiff of someone else's mortality mixed up in the stink of danger. The urge to turn away is strong, but not half as powerful as the compulsion to watch. The officers began a slow, methodical search of the man's jeep, keeping at least one weapon trained on him at all times. This scene plays itself out like a movie: a bad slasher flick that repels you more than scares you. But at least the drama ends with a whimper, not a bang.

If you come from a country where firearms don't have a place in polite company, you are much more sensitised to a telling show of power like this one. It taunts you into all kinds of generalisations about race, guns and policing in America. But past mistakes tell me that the easy judgement is not always the right one.

The police seemed professional. There was no brutality. Perhaps there was just cause for the drawn guns. If so, is there really a moral to the story? Perhaps it is simply this: the Sunbelt is still the frontier. For all the comforting rituals of the firehouse, people here still look to a sheriff with a gun.

This an exceptional place where people have it all and so have everything to lose. The only guarantee of peace of mind on the frontier is the strict observance of the rituals that bind neighbours to the harsh enforcement of the rules that protect citizens against strangers. Safety in a town like Gilbert requires that bad things happen to bad people.

It has always been this way on the frontier, in fact as well as in fiction. In one of the first popular novels of American literature, *The Pioneers*, a central character, Judge Marmaduke Temple, explains the impatient strain of Western justice: 'Living as we do, gentlemen, on the skirts of society, it becomes doubly necessary to protect the ministers of the law.'

The same exacting standards govern relationships between

individuals. In the movie *The Shootist*, John Wayne plays a lone gunfighter reflecting on the philosophy of a hard, frontier life: 'I won't be wronged. I won't be insulted. I won't be laid-a-hand on. I don't do these things to other people, and I require the same from them.'

The frontier offers a personal space over which you are promised absolute control, but to guard that fiercely prized independence, pioneers need an extreme level of security. In the wrong circumstances, that combination turns the tension between Frontier and Ritual into a self-destructive spiral. Instead of the good balancing the bad, the worst aspects of the two personalities began to reinforce themselves. Reaction begets over-reaction.

Few issues reveal that dysfunction better than the debate over guns. The absolute right to bear arms in the United States has become mixed up with an obssessional desire for security. The result is a dangerous, and often farcical, contradiction.

Right next to Gilbert, in the constellation of boomburbs that surrounds Phoenix, are the cities of Chandler and Mesa. In late August 2007, officials at Payne Junior High School in Chandler suspended a 13-year-old boy for making a very rough sketch of a gun. Mindful of events such as the Columbine massacre of 1999, the school said that the boy posed a real threat to his classmates.

Just a few months later, the State Senator for Mesa, Karen Johnson, proposed a bill in the Arizona legislature to allow teachers and students over 21 to carry their concealed weapons into schools and universities. Johnson wanted to give law-abiding individuals the right to defend themselves against a weirdo on the rampage. 'We are not the wild, wild West like people think we are,' Johnson said, 'but people are more independent thinkers here when it comes to security.'

Just think. To protect lives, school officials suspend a 13-year-old boy from school for sketching a gun. To protect lives, a local politician says that concealed weapons should be carried into schools. Individuals demand the right to bear arms, while communities demand protection from misfits with guns. More guns means more death. More death begets harsher rules and more guns.

You have to wonder about America's future when you see this kind of spectacular spiral play itself out in the sedate desert boomburbs of Gilbert, Chandler and Mesa. The civic pride of the firefighters told us that we were in the most forward-looking and optimistic place in the United States, but politics here is still flavoured by the sour taste of history. Even as the Sunbelt is being transformed, it still battles the savage, self-destructive instincts of the earliest American frontier.

—•—

The Sunbelt *is* the Wild West, give or take a century or two. From the Mojave Desert to the Gulf of Mexico, the legends of the original frontier are never far from people's minds. But you don't hear much about the grubby, brutish and harsh place the Wild West was before Hollywood got its hands on it.

The first great Westering wave of movement in the 19th century was a chance for the little man to escape from the ruling elite, whether that was feudal landlords in the old country or Yankee nabobs back East. It is easy to eulogise these early pioneers but the freedom many of them sought was shallow and savage.

In their book *Frontiers*, Robert Hine and John Mack Faragher say: 'If freedom is defined by the absence of external restraint, then they were a supreme example of free men … but if freedom is a state of mind, it is arguable that men like this were maladjusted, and their aversion to society was based on a restless pursuit of something they could neither find nor define.'

Individual freedom was not an ideal in early frontier days. It was a commodity to be jealously guarded. But as the West began to assume increasing importance, American opinion-makers cast an ideological cloak to cover the naked grab for land, power and personal enrichment. So was born the doctrine of 'manifest destiny', which elevated the expansion of the United States to the status of a divine mission.

The frontier also spawned a type of rough and ready politician who would shape the political culture of the Wild West – 'men with the bark on', as the artist Frederic Remington put it. Some came from the Southern states laden down with prejudice and rebellion. The legendary Davy Crockett made the move from Tennessee to Texas in 1836 only after his political career there had stalled. 'I told the people of my district that if they saw fit to elect me, I would serve them faithfully,' he told a crowd. 'But if not, they might go to hell and I would go to Texas. I was beaten, gentlemen, and here I am.'

The rough frontier ethic was shaped in large measure by Ulster Protestant immigrants (who would become known as the Scots-Irish). They initially made landfall in the South, but their influence would spread as America expanded West. Perhaps the most famous Scots-Irish politician was Andrew Jackson. 'Old Hickory', as he was known, first gained prominence battling Indian tribes in Tennessee at the turn of the 19th century. In 1828, he was elected the seventh president of the United States.

Nobody messes with the descendants of Andrew Jackson. You are with them or you or against them. If you believe one of Jackson's early biographers, that certainty was forged in Ireland: 'It appears to be more difficult for a North-of-Irelander than for other men to allow an honest difference of opinion in an opponent'.

'Jacksonian' is a term that American political scientists apply to the aggressively nationalistic strand in American life. In his book *America Right or Wrong*, Anatol Lieven offers a particularly harsh (and perhaps simplistic) assessment of the link between

Jacksonian tradition and Ulster Protestants, 'who after settling Ulster and largely exterminating its Gaelic Irish Catholic population, later brought their fundamentalist Protestantism and their ruthless warfare with them to the Americas'.

The Jacksonian tradition was carried along the advancing frontier by leaders like John C. Calhoun and Sam Houston. The nationalism of these Scots-Irish pioneers was writ especially large in Texas, which provided fertile ground for values of 'toughness, maleness and whiteness in defence of family, race and nation'.

The unforgiving quality of Texas life finds expression in a uniquely sharp sense of humour. In his exceptional book *People of Paradox*, Michael Kammen offers us this example, taken from the sign over a hotel in an old Texas frontier town:

> *Come to Van Horn to live.*
> *The climate is so healthy,*
> *We had to shoot a man*
> *To start our graveyard.*

In case you think the dubious frontier psyche was fashioned solely by Ulster Protestants, think again. Immigrants from all parts of Ireland played a part. In his evocative book *How the Irish Won the West*, Myles Dungan captures the spectrum of instincts which drove these Irish frontier-men – and -women –from the humanity of public servants like Thomas Fitzpatrick, the drive and courage of businesswoman Nellie Cashman, all the way to the savagery of Indian-killer Jim Kirker, who collected $200 for the scalps of every one of the 500 Apache warriors he hunted down in Mexico and New Mexico.

Some believe that these Irish-Americans were brutalised by their own desire for respect and belonging. The Irish had arrived in America to find that they were looked down on by the Yankee establishment of the East coast. It would take generations for the Irish to prove that they were real Americans. Anatol Lieven says that 'Irish-Americans sought to overcome their exclusion not only through militant nationalism but specifically through being "First in War".'

Whether they created it or not, the Irish and Scots-Irish were in the vanguard of a fiercely traditional and rebellious conservatism that would shape the American Southwest. 'Frontier days in Texas are not so far in the past,' wrote author Warren Leslie in the 1960s. 'The man who fights, who resists trespass, who takes no orders from groups or from other men and who will not compromise – this is the frontier man, and he is still around in Dallas, and in Texas.'

Above all else, the politics of the frontier produced mavericks like Senator Barry Goldwater of Arizona, the man credited with the renaissance of American conservatism. He became a national figure in the early 1960s, and extolled the virtues of the Sunbelt, where he said 'individual initiative made the desert bloom'. His manifesto, *The Consience of a Conservative*, popularised a distinctly Western brand of conservatism with an emphasis on self-reliance, hostility to government and devout anti-communism.

Goldwater lost the 1964 presidential election to Lyndon Johnson, but his ideas guided a movement that carried another Sunbelt conservative, Ronald Reagan, to the White House, and inspired the conservative revolution that redrew the American political map. That realignment has given the Republican Party victory in seven out ten presidential elections since 1968.

In their portrait of America's conservative movement, *The Right Nation*, John Micklethwaite and Adrian Wooldridge describe how the early Sunbelt suburbs influenced American political culture: 'These Westerners were natural individualists: people who lived in bungalows, not apartment blocks, and who relied on cars rather than public transport … and they judged people usually by what they achieved rather than where they came from.'

It is no exaggeration to say that the last great realignment of American politics began in the Sunbelt four decades ago. Now, the American West is about to play a super-sized part in the next realignment. The population explosion that came with the Great Dispersal means that states like Texas, California, Nevada and Arizona are gaining more seats in the US Congress and more votes in the electoral college that chooses the president.

The Sunbelt is a gathering storm with the power to reshape American politics, but how will it use that power? Does the bitter, hard-edged traditions of the frontier still drive the most dynamic part of America?

In short, just how damn conservative are the boomburbs?

—•—

To answer that question, we have to revisit our Frontier and Ritual formula. As pioneers on a Frontier begin to settle, they tend to move toward the moderating influence of Ritual. That gradual journey is exactly what is happening on the Sunbelt Frontier right now. The evidence suggests that as the boomburbs settle, and civic rituals take root, citizens begin to move away from the hard edge of frontier conservatism and towards the political centre. The political loyalties of the boomburbs are increasingly up for grabs, with voters evenly balanced between the Republican and Democratic parties, particularly at local level.

In national elections, the boomburb voter has become a swing voter. When George Bush first ran for president in 2000, he and his opponent Al Gore won an equal number of the counties containing boomburbs. In 2004, he won 15 out of 26, but his margin of victory was relatively small in most cases.

The 2004 election did expose a difference between the more settled boomburbs, which have passed the manic phase of their expansion, and suburbs which are still growing rapidly. In 2004, 97 of America's 100 fastest-growing suburbs backed George Bush, which suggests that those boomburbs and baby-boomburbs which retain that disorderly frontier quality tend to be more conservative.

However, theirs is a different strain of conservatism. No longer do individual pursuits make the desert bloom. Today, even at the most frantic stretch of the Sunbelt Frontier, the spirit of the collective has increasing influence over political sympathies.

This change in political culture is at least partly explained by the rise of a highly participatory form of self-rule in boomburbs. More and more Sunbelt neighbourhoods are controlled by 'homeowners associations', which act like private governments. They raise their own revenue and contract in essential services like refuse collection and maintenance. They also set the rules which govern public life in their neighbourhood.

If boomburb residents have to look for help outside their master-planned communities, they look only as far as City Hall. Municipal government is run by part-time elected officials with the same fierce commitment to self-reliance and participation. If they need another school or firehouse, they hold a referendum and vote to float a bond.

There are broader risks with this kind of privatised democracy (which we will come back to later), but clearly it has positive elements. Most importantly, it helps to revive the civic engagement which many believed the suburbs had killed off. It also takes the hard edge off political culture.

Linda Talbott is an elected member of the Gilbert town council and a mirror to the city's soul. Vivacious and tactile, you could not have been a better advertisement for the social charm of boomburb living. She came to Gilbert from Georgia 20 years ago, and is a zealous advocate for the evolving traditions shaping America's fastest-growing city. To Linda, tradition does not necessarily mean the narrow, religious morality we have come to associate with American conservatism. 'I would describe myself as socially liberal and fiscally conservative,' she says, 'I am a capitalist.'

Gilbert is barren ground for extreme ideas of any kind. People here are well-read and well-off; the average resident of Gilbert is significantly more educated and richer than the Arizona average. They work in a variety of premium business positions, either located inside the city or in nearby boomburbs. For many, the primary business in Gilbert is having and raising kids. Linda tells me with inordinate pride that Gilbert has a younger population than the American average, and has higher fertility and marriage rates than anywhere in Arizona. 'An average of four children per woman,' she claims.

For all its vitality, Gilbert remains insulated from many of the traditions that have driven previous American reinventions, such as the impact of diversity. The number of African-Americans and foreign-born people who live here is significantly lower than in the rest of Arizona. Gilbert speaks of dynamism, optimism and moderation, but also of retreat. When it comes to politics, Gilbert seems to be missing the progressive gene.

Gilbert and Surprise were good to George W. Bush. Initially, these boomburbs were attracted to him less for his classic Frontier sensibility than his promise of Ritual, expressed in that slogan 'compassionative conservatism'. He could not have won in places like Gilbert unless he came across as moderate and optimistic. In 2004, Gilbert and its surrounding county backed Bush for a second time, after he stirred up the kind of frontier fears which resonated with communities still 'on the skirts of society'.

However, by 2008, a backlash was developing along the Sunbelt Frontier. Bush's second term had managed to disillusion committed Republicans like Linda Talbott. Even in the rapidly growing suburbs like Gilbert, the prevailing wind was blowing against the Republicans.

A maverick from Arizona, an optimistic conservative with a smallish 'c', John McCain was the living, breathing example of how much frontier conservatism has been transformed by the sunny rituals of the Sunbelt.

—•—

It is 2 February, the Saturday before 'Super Tuesday' and one of the gatekeepers of California conservatism, John Fleischman, is about to talk to Senator John McCain. Fleischman is in his bare feet, sitting on a stool in his kitchen with the phone to his ear and two laptop computers open on the small round table in front of him.

The blinds are drawn but the sunshine seems to curl around the wooden slats. John is wearing a rumpled check sleeveless shirt with a button-down collar. His youthful, rounded face looks fresh, but there are signs that it may have been a late night in the Fleischman household. The sink is filled with dirty dishes and there's an open bottle of red wine near the fridge with perhaps another glass and a half left in it.

It's early afternoon and John's wife and five-month-old baby boy are asleep upstairs in their apartment in the nondescript Orange County suburb of Irvine. The modest surroundings are misleading. John Fleischman is a smart guy. He sold his original house and rented this apartment just before the bottom fell out of the property market in Orange County. John still feels the market has some way to go before it hits absolute rock-bottom, so he will spend a few more months in this apartment with his family.

John Fleischman is vice-chairman of the Republican Party in southern California, but that is not why John McCain is about to speak to him. He has influence because he is the publisher of the state's leading conservative website, the *Flash Report*. If you need to get to the Californians who think Ronald Reagan is a god and Hillary Clinton is the devil's spawn, you have to go through John Fleischman. He is the keeper of the flame, defender of Orange County's proud tradition as a lighthouse of Western conservative values in California's broad, deep liberal ocean.

John makes a decent living. As well as the advertising revenue from his website, he is a sought-after speaker and gets paid by corporations who want to raise their profile among well-connected conservatives. He is engaged and lacks the suspicion you expect of a zealot, but he has a reputation as a hard-liner.

'The more crazy and right-wing I am,' he says, 'the better it is for business.'

The confessional small-talk comes to an abrupt end when he hears a voice on the other end of the phone.

'Hello, Senator. It's John Fleischman. We're just going to ask you a few questions for our podcast. Shouldn't take more than a few minutes.'

'Thank you, John. I'm glad to be with you.'

Of course he is. This is California: 40 million people. One in eight Americans. Super Tuesday's glittering prize.

McCain is a comedian. He has a line in self-deprecating wit that never fails to charm, no matter how many times you have heard it.

'Listen, I know California has been stealing Arizona's water,' he says with a smile in his voice, 'and I know my fellow Phoenicians are mistreated and called Zonies when they cross over into San Diego, but I know the issues that affect the West and I will work in California and I will win in California.'

The big question is the war in Iraq. To liberals, it has been a murderous failure. To conservatives, it is unfinished business. John Fleischman lobs a soft-ball.

'A lot of our readers are trying to understand the distinction between a war to stop terrorism and a war to bring democracy to Iraq. Could you just speak to that for a moment?'

McCain criticised the Bush administration for bungling the reconstruction of Iraq, but he also risked political annihilation by backing the 'surge' strategy. Both those maverick stands seem to have paid off, and have been the cornerstones of McCain's remarkable comeback. Rather than being trapped by an unpopular war, McCain is liberated by it. It gives him the chance to appeal to all sides in his own party while stamping on both candidates for the Democratic Party nomination.

'If we do what Senator Clinton and Senator Obama want to do and wave the white flag of surrender, my friends, we will be fighting not just there but in other places in the world because al-Qaeda will have won. And that is just a fact.'

There is an angry quality in McCain's voice as he utters those last words. You feel that he believes it, but you also feel that he is straining to reach people like John Fleischman. Among the conservative faithful in Orange County, McCain is a hard sell. He simply isn't a true believer. He may have come from the Sunbelt, but he is not of the frontier. He is no Ronald Reagan, and certainly no Barry Goldwater.

For for a few moments after his interview, Fleischman ponders what he has heard from McCain. In that tiny kitchen with the dirty dishes and drawn blinds, he focusses on the tough talk about Iraq.

'A lot of Republicans want a guy in the White House who will finish the job, who will make sure that every Islamic fundamentalist terrorist out there in the world realises that if they beat up on us or any of our allies, including the fine folks in Ireland, they will pay a price to do it.'

This is foreign policy spoken with the accent of Andrew Jackson, Reagan and Bush. John McCain can do a fair imitation, but you get the feeling that Scarytalk is his second language. He knows he has to sell some fear here in Orange County, yet not as much as he probably thinks.

—•—

Driving into Ladera Ranch is like slipping into a warm bath. The 4,000-acre master-planned suburb doesn't quite sprawl; it seeps inexorably across the foothills of the Saddleback mountains near Mission Viejo like a rising tide of goodness and warmth.

There are differences you notice about Ladera Ranch the moment you drive through the first traffic barrier (open by day, closed by night). The first is the roundabout. It is traditionally an alien concept in Orange County and all across America because it requires drivers to have faith in the good judgement of an approaching stranger. Perhaps in such an ostentatiously close community, the stranger will turn out to be a neighbour, but driving through that roundabout is like falling backwards into someone else's arms; it requires a level of civic trust you would not have found in suburban America a generation ago.

As you go deeper into the community, the streets seem to get narrower. Everything feels more intimate. Ladera Ranch is divided into villages and neighbourhoods, all either respectably affluent or modestly rich. A group of ten or more villages is called a neighbourhood. At the heart of each village is a clubhouse, which is designed to reflect a different architectural theme. All around the clubhouse are parks, pools, playgrounds and open areas. The phrase 'housing development' doesn't even come close to capturing its essence. Ladera Ranch did not develop. It was conceived.

Back in 1999, before a single house was built, the promoters of Ladera Ranch sent out surveys to 20,000 people who had responded to a billboard campaign along the freeways of Orange County. Some of the questions were eminently predictable, asking people to choose between playing fields and nature trails.

There were slightly more intrusive questions which asked respondents to rate the importance of life goals like 'making it big' or 'finding your purpose in life'. But when prospective buyers reached the section entitled 'values', it was clear they weren't being sold just any old suburb.

The questions asked people to rate how strongly they agreed with various statements. 'We need to treat the planet as a living system,' read one. 'Abortions should not be legal unless there's a threat to life,' read another. It also asked people to agree or disagree with the declaration: 'I have been born again in Jesus Christ.' There were questions about corporate greed, divorce, foreign travel and the pros and cons of 'experiencing exotic people or places'.

As Ladera Ranch took shape, the survey allowed the marketers to divide potential buyers into 'values subcultures' and to socially engineer the villages and neighbourhoods that made up the new community. The more conservative-minded buyers (labelled the 'traditionalists') were directed towards the Covenant Hills neighbourhood where homes had classic architecture and big family rooms and cost anything up to $5 million. The more liberal, socially aware 'Cultural Creatives' were led in the direction of Terramor, where houses are fitted with photovoltaic cells and bamboo flooring. Other categories of new homeowners included status-conscious 'winners' and 'winners with heart'.

The designers of the Ladera Ranch could not care less whether the people who live in their community are muesli-eating lefties or bible-bashing conservatives, but they correctly understood that on the Sunbelt Frontier, the selling point of any master-planned community is how it 'feels'.

The people who move to these developments have far bigger expectations of the suburbs than their parents once had. They are looking for more than a way of life which simply supplies job, house, money and class. They want to surround themselves with a style of life shaped by their own personal preferences in architecture and colour, sport and music, faith and politics.

To meet that desire, developers have to rely on a branch of social research called psychographics. Where demographic research tells you about people on the basis of their age, race and sex, psychographics tells you about their attitudes, personalities and values.

'We were trying to characterize the lens through which people see the world,' said Brooke Warrick, who heads the marketing firm that sold Ladera Ranch. 'A community is a collection of symbols and images, and we wanted our symbols and images to be better than the other guy's.'

As a marketing exercise, Ladera Ranch was a big success and is now home to more than 20,000 people, but as an experiment in social engineering it was less accomplished. One resident of the 'culturally creative' and environmentally sensitive enclave of Terramor told a journalist from the *Washington Post* that a neighbour had turned his so-called 'culture room' into a TV room with a 50-inch screen. Another had installed a big swimming pool and $100,000 worth of landscaping. 'The truth is, I got a neighbor with a Hummer. I doubt he's very soul-searching.'

Still, almost ten years after it was built, Ladera Ranch speaks eloquently of the lives of the people who live on the Sunbelt Frontier. The various neighbourhoods still look like miniature versions of the shining city, radiating contentment and well-being. If there is one dark cloud hanging over this image of perfection, it is the rapid slide of the property market. Back in 2006, the price of the average home in the community had reached $1.5 million. By the end of 2007, it had fallen back to $1 million, and by April 2008, it was descending rapidly toward the $750,000 mark.

In spite of that insecurity (and perhaps because of it), Ladera Ranch is like Gilbert, Arizona, in that its speaks of a revival of civic life and a more optimistic conservatism. It reflects the political sensibilities of Orange County, with 'traditonalists' outnumbering 'cultural creatives' (the local records show political donations in this area heavily favour the Republican Party). But it is even younger, richer and better educated than its Arizona counterpart. Unlike Gilbert, it reflects America's growing diversity: more than one in four people who live there are either Asian or Latino, and more than one in three is drawn from some ethnic minority.

Ladera Ranch offers a valuable insight into the emerging political culture of Sunbelt suburbia. The citizens of these communities do not want to be segregated into ghettos based on either ethnic background or 'values subcultures'. They want to make a statement about their lives, but they do not want to be defined by race or politics. When they choose a new community, they make a grand statement about what type of society they want their kids to grow up in. When they come to a place like Ladera Ranch, they trade a narrow, static definition of suburban values for the optimistic, interactive and diverse culture of boomburbia, but they take their traditions with them as they head down the freeway. They want change, but they don't do risk. After all, they are the ones feeling the pinch of a faltering economy. The frontier they live on is still conservative, but not in the way we might have expected.

—•—

Noah McMahon stands beside the sleek silver Land Rover in the driveway of his elegant Tuscan-style house and guides us in. He appreciates how easy it is for visitors to get lost in the warren of culs-de-sac that make up Covenant Hills. Noah makes it clear on the phone that people in Ladera Ranch no longer take all that talk of social engineering seriously. But, for the record, he is a 'traditionalist'.

Noah once worked for Richard Nixon. In the 2008 election cycle, he donated the maximum individual contribution of

$2,300 to Mitt Romney, the solid social conservative in the race for the Republican nomination. When I bring up Rick Warren and the nearby Saddleback Church, Noah uses the phrase 'fundamentalist Christian' to describe himself. But at the very same time, there's something worldly and cosmopolitan about him, despite his beard, saggy jeans, olive green shirt and fundamentalist Christianity. In the open stone kitchen of his house, he introduces his wife Debbie and their two young daughters, Sydney and Shawna. The conversation turns to travel, and Debbie tells me the kids travelled the world with their parents. Shawna recounts the story of her most recent trip to Majorca with the trademark politeness and confidence of a well-bred American pre-teen.

When Noah starts to talk about his business interests, it's hard to keep up. First, there is his marketing and events management company with a celebrity client list ranging from the Beach Boys to skateboard legend Tony Hawk. Noah's primary contract is for the relaunch of one of the biggest casinos in Las Vegas. Then there is his other company, Zero-G, specialising in 'space entertainment and tourism'. It is the only commercial operation offering the experience of weightlessness. It has flown its customers (including Tom Hanks and Stephen Hawking) into lunar, martian and zero-gravity on board a specially designed jet called G-Force One.

But enough about space; we are here to talk about politics. It is 2 February and Super Tuesday is just days away. Noah is hosting a small, intimate gathering of Gen-Next, a network of young professionals based in Orange County. The group has no explicitly partisan agenda, but it is mainstream conservative and solidly Republican.

Noah's fellow members arrive a few minutes late. Michael Davidson works full-time for Gen-Next and has a certain youthful star quality. He cut his teeth as a conservative activist on the fiercely liberal campus of Berkeley University and was a national leader of America's college Republican movement. He seems destined for great things and is already heavily involved in Arnold Schwarzenegger's campaign to win another term as Governor of California.

Dave Luzuriaga is a successful engineer with no clear Republican pedigree. He proves to be the most ideologically thoughtful of the group. He talks with passion about his father coming from Ecuador to embrace the American dream. 'I'm here because I am a big believer in capitalism,' he says.

Within minutes, all three men have staked out their priorities in the approaching election. Dave begins by saying 'I am a firm believer that the Republican Party needs to be moderate.' When it's time for Noah to speak, I expect him to disagree and opt for that frontier tradition of conservatism. But what comes out of his mouth is criticism of President Bush and his mishandling of the nation's finances. 'When it comes to spending money,' he says, 'Bush wasn't very conservative.'

All three agree that the big issue facing Orange County in the coming election is the economic insecurity people here feel in their bones. 'February has just been the worst month,' Noah says with a chilling emphasis.

But the harsh realities of the economy are quickly dispensed with as the three young conservatives list their priorities. Again, it is Noah who surprises the most. 'You know, I take the long view, and that's why ecological issues matter to me,' he says, unprovoked. 'People say that conservatives don't care about environmental issues, but we do.'

Dave talks of his frustration at the rapid disintegration of his country's standing in the world, saying it 'deeply saddens me what has happened under Bush and Cheney'. As a moderate, as the son of an immigrant, you would expect Dave to be more conscious of the global missteps of the Bush administration. But both Michael and Noah see mistakes made and chances missed during the previous eight years.

'Candidates like Mitt Romney and John McCain got the message in this election,' Michael says. 'We didn't appreciate the way leaders squandered a conservative opportunity. We need to change.'

Noah, Michael and David show no sign of deserting the Republican Party. But they speak for that vast swathe of young traditionalists who have helped to colonise the Sunbelt Frontier. They want the best of the past, but they have come to hate the demagogues of the right who claim to speak in the name of Goldwater and Reagan. They are looking for a more civic-minded conservatism that is less tribal and more open to the world. 'Moderate' is not the best word. 'Pragmatic' is better. They are looking for Republicans who can move with the changing lifestyles of younger Americans. What they want is a leader who can speak with authenticity on issues which defy existing political difference – issues like the environment.

Make no mistake, these three men have nothing but disdain for the Democrats. If fact, their hatred of Hillary Clinton borders on mania. Fear of another Clinton presidency has helped to focus their minds in the run-up to Super Tuesday. Even Noah, the most traditional of the three, has decided to switch support from Romney to McCain: 'I think Mitt Romney would be terrific for so many reasons,' he says, 'but I will support John McCain because I think he is more electable. Let's just hope Hillary gets the nomination on the other side.'

'It's about defining the art of losing the battle to win the war,' says Dave the moderate, 'so I'm with Noah on that.'

'I try to be fairly consistent about my conservative values,' says Michael. 'But what would happen if we lost all our conservative philosophy to Hillary Clinton?'

There is the possibility that these three very different conservatives are united by fear. In the face of that collapsing economy and the plummeting value of their houses, they are looking for a temporary reprieve, not a transformation.

Maybe it is pessimism, not optimism, that is moderating the conservatism of the Sunbelt.

But more than any other group, the young conservatives of Orange County anticipate a transformation. Their lifestyles and businesses are built around innovation. They may express gloom about the way the country is going but they are sincerely optimistic about their own lives. And that is why they are looking for a new type of conservative, someone ready to shift the balance slowly, carefully away from old notions of Frontier, towards the safety of Ritual.

The three men all have commitments. They need to leave as soon as our conversation is over. Dave is rushing back to see his kid's softball game. Noah is off to view two properties deeper into Covenant Hills that he is interested in buying as an investment. Michael is on the prowl for property and even though the million-plus asking price is out of his league, he asks Noah if he can come. When I ask if it really is a good time to be buying houses, they both look at me in surprise, as if I hadn't been listening properly.

'I am very optimistic,' says Noah with patience. 'It's just going to take a conservative to sort this out.' And I think I know exactly what kind of conservative he means.

If all you had seen were Gilbert and Ladera Ranch, you would have cleared out your savings account, raided the kids' piggybanks, and bet everything on John McCain. The soft suburban conservatism of Linda Talbott and Noah McMahon is a powerful force on the Sunbelt Frontier, and there is no doubt it will have a hand in shaping America after Bush's presidency. But there is another quickening wind blowing across that frontier. We got a hint at the football game in Saguaro, in the faces of a new generation – a transformational generation.

Part Two:
The Generation

4.
Brownsville – The Joshua Generation

Everybody loves a parade, but this one is beyond beautiful. Even the man employed to shovel the horse shit off Elizabeth Street seems a little misty-eyed as he contemplates the spectacular grace of it all. The women on horseback in front of him are dressed in colours so vivid, they may leave a permanent imprint on his retinas. The lead rider is a blaze of glossy tangerine ruffles running from her chin all the way to her tiptoes. She is wearing an inscrutable smirk like the young woman who follows her. On her head is a wide-brimmed sombrero turned up at the back. It is hard to make out the detail of her face, but, when she turns her head, the shadow disappears and the colours of her dress are reflected onto her skin. Amber and lime. Sublime.

The horses keep walking and the women are soon gone. They are heading for the bridge that spans the Rio Grande. It connects Brownsville on the US side with its twin city of Matamoros in Mexico. Locals tell you that this is the only parade that starts in one country and ends in another. It happens once a year during a festival called Charro Days, and celebrates the collision of Mexican and American culture which shapes life here in south Texas. In other parts of the West, you use the word Latino to describe those with Latin and South American roots. Here it is Mexican-American or Hispanic.

The crowd along the parade route is five and six deep in

places. The early birds sit out in front on folding chairs munching Frito Pies, a sloppily delicious concoction of chilli and tortilla chips. Happy gangs of people are perched on the upstairs balconies of the weather-beaten wooden houses along Elizabeth Street. Each passing display is greeted with the same generous roar of approval: the boys in a Mariachi band; more horses and riders; an enormous inflatable bottle of Tecate beer; another Mariachi band; portly old men from the local Shriner chapter riding miniature motorcycles; a high school marching band; a local radio host surrounded by dancing girls in short pants; the next marching band; Mexican cowboys on horseback; the man with the shovel.

The even-handed cheer turns into a collective roar when a long red convertible appears with police officers running by its side. It carries the parade's guest of honour, Angelica Vale, the star of the hit Mexican telenovela *La Fea Más Bella*. The finale of her show was one of the most-watched Spanish-language broadcasts in US history. She may be unknown to a wider world, but she is a celebrity of the very highest order in this town.

The frenzied roar dies down as the convertible passes. The crowd seems a little exhausted by the outpouring of worship and politely applaud a series of cars carrying local dignitaries. But as a vintage jeep comes into view, the applause gets warmer and louder. Sitting together on the back seat of the vehicle are State Senator Eddie Lucio, Jr and his son, State Representative Eddie Lucio III, stalwarts of the Democratic Party in south Texas.

The word 'dynasty' does not do justice to the Lucio family. The cheers that you hear from the crowd tell you that these men have a connection with their electorate that most politicians can only dream of. They don't just represent people here; they reflect their aspirations. Like the firehouses of Gilbert, they anchor a community which has been on the wrong side of the frontier, even if it is on the American side of the border.

Eddie Senior has been a public representative for almost forty years, yet he doesn't look old enough. He has had some health problems and is hard of hearing in one ear but any fair-minded stranger would put him in his early fifties. He is neat, almost dapper. His thick black hair is parted with precision. He speaks with a rich baritone and the hint of an accent.

Eddie Lucio grew up in a small house in Brownsville with his five brothers and four sisters. His father fought in World War II and was injured twice during the Americans' gruelling advance through Italy. A powerful, uncomplicated strand of patriotism has been handed down from father to son. 'My dad was a disabled veteran,' Eddie says, 'and he preached citizenship and American-ness to us. He told us, even though we were Mexican-American, we should never hyphenate who we were.'

But Eddie learned another lesson from his elders about the brutality of life in the early frontier days. Mexican-Americans were often victims of those 'Jacksonian' settlers who came to tame the new border territory, including members of the Texas Rangers, the now celebrated citizen militia. Eddie's grandfather was forced to flee into Mexico after witnessing the killing of a local farmer by a Ranger who wanted his land.

Life in Brownsville still has a hard edge to it, but clearly the Lucios have come a very long way since the bad old days. To get to the Senator's home, you travel ten miles out of Brownsville into the flat, tropical scrub on either side of San Marcos Road. At the appointed turn, you follow a street full of trailer homes and small, boxy bungalows. It leads you to a set of electronic gates with the distinctive Texas star in the middle. In the circle around the star are the words 'Senator Lucio'. Behind the gates is a causeway which leads across a lake to the Senator's six-acre retreat.

Besides politics, Eddie Lucio's big passion is golf. One of his brothers is a professional at a local course and between them they run a company that builds golf carts. Sitting behind the wheel of one of those carts, Eddie's early reticence slips away and he leads you on a captivating journey through his faith and his family. He is deeply religious and has the stations of the cross posted on timber frames along the five-mile stretch of pathway that winds around his land. He talks about idyllic warm summer evenings out on that lake with his wife. They will take a glass of wine on to a pontoon boat and sit and listen to the sound of the birds in the thick canopy of trees and bushes.

Eddie Lucio's is a success story. He is a symbol of power, influence and public service. He says that local schoolchildren were asked to name their public representatives and when each position was called out – Congressman, Senator, Governor – they kept repeating the name 'Eddie Lucio'. But, despite all the pride, I detect in him a hint of ambivalence or perhaps a touch of weariness.

Eddie tells me a strange story. At a civic reception, a man approached him. 'I could see the way he was sizing me up that he was trouble,' he says. 'He came up and said "I don't like you." After a pause he told me, "But I will vote for you because you helped my father."' It turns out that Eddie had stopped and helped an old man who had a flat tyre and no jack. It was the man's father. 'That is politics in south Texas,' he says with a not-all-that-comfortable smile.

Eddie Lucio pulls the golf cart in front of the house and leads me into the kitchen where we meet his son. Eddie Junior comes across as the kind of man who is permanently in transit. This morning, he left his house without having breakfast. Even as he is introducing himself, he is opening the door to the pantry and helping himself to a cereal bar and a diet soda. But he has a rare knack that you see only in the very best politicians: the ability to make a genuine, human connection in spite of a short attention span. He asks questions and consider the answers, never breaks eye contact when he is speaking, and is respectfully silent when his father talks, yet he is not afraid to pick him up on something when he disagrees.

Eddie Junior was elected to the State legislature two years ago, at the age of twenty-seven. He has the looks and attitude of a star athlete, which is not surprising since he almost made it as a professional golfer. 'It just didn't work out,' he says with finality. He went back to law school in the state capital, Austin, and thought long and hard about his future. Explaining why he finally chose politics, he says: 'I saw the way people would look at my father. I heard the things he had done for them.'

Eddie's father admits that the Lucio name played a role in his eventual election but says his son deserves most of the credit. 'He beat two really experienced attorneys. Anyway, the family name might help you get in the first time, but it takes hard work the second time.' As we walk into the garden, the father leans in close and says: 'He will be Governor of Texas. I have no doubt.'

Down at the water's edge, the two men begin to talk about the presidential election campaign. Voters across Texas will choose between Barack Obama and Hillary Clinton in a few days time, and both the Lucios are prized gatekeepers to the Hispanic community. Close as they are, these two men are on opposite sides of a defining political battle. The father is backing Hillary Clinton, while his son is supporting Barack Obama.

'My son and I have a difference of opinion on the presidency,' says the older man. 'My judgement is based on the fact that I have known Hillary Clinton since her husband ran for president. I know them and they know our struggles. Eddie can speak for himself.'

The younger man doesn't need an invitation. His rhetoric has a slightly more packaged feel than his father's, but there is no less passion.

'If was basing my support on who I was loyal to, I would go with the Clintons. I had my Bill Clinton T-shirt when he was running back in '92. But right now, with so much at stake, we really need to look at who is best for America.'

Policy has nothing to do with the disagreement between

93

father and son. It is all about the personality of the politics they each embody. Life has taught the father that you don't get anywhere without paying your dues, showing respect to your elders and never flinching in the face of your enemies.

'I want to look at experience and when someone comes to me and says "I want the most important job in the country," I want to make sure that someone is seasoned, that it is someone who has never walked away from a fight. I am describing Hillary Clinton.'

The son has learned a different lesson. Times have changed in south Texas. A new generation is on the rise in America. Move with the times or move over.

'We have had twenty years of the same and we need someone who will show the world that America is changing its course. It's important that we have that once-in-a-generation candidate. That's who I believe Obama is.'

If the father is irritated by the presumptuousness of his son's choice, he doesn't show it. Instead, there's something almost unbearably poignant about what he says next.

'My once-in-a-lifetime candidate was gunned down. It was Bobby Kennedy. I cried and cried for a long time when he was no longer around. I felt like Eddie did, that he was the rising star that America needed, but you know …'

Then the father is back to his riff about Hillary Clinton's experience and strength. But it is hard to concentrate on what he is saying. The image of this hard-grafting veteran politician, as a young man, closing the door of his room and crying after the assassination of his generation's shining hope is too raw.

It is not the first time I have heard this searing sense of loss from a man of Eddie Lucio's age and political inclination. Just weeks before, a liberal small-town mayor in Iowa called Jerry Kelley had told me how more than a few townsmen had phoned him to say the same thing. 'They told me they were in Vietnam when Bobby Kennedy was killed. They were denied their chance to vote for a transformational leader back then. They never got it again. Not until now, with Obama.'

But the older Lucio reveals the flip-side of the same coin. He is a pragmatic man who believes that there is no second coming in American politics. His generation's chance has passed. It is foolish to pretend otherwise. Beware of false prophets from another generation, he seems to say, and stick with what you know.

You hear a similar expression of wounded frustration from women of Eddie's age who fought the battles that hardened Hillary Clinton. As the Pulitzer-prizewinning columnist Ellen Goodman has put it: 'Sexism, slurs and struggles wore grooves down their memory lanes.' Now they see women of their daughters' generation rejecting a pioneer of the struggle in favour of a slick young man with no experience. The comparison of Obama to Bobby Kennedy is an insult. Hell no, these veterans seem to say, if Bobby was alive today, he'd be voting for Hillary.

If any such bitterness has crept into the Lucio family, both father and son are anxious to defuse it. They reach across to grab each other's shoulders or arms and begin as many sentences as possible with the phrases, 'I agree with Eddie …' or 'My father is right.'

'We are colleagues and we are family,' the son assures me. 'We mind those relationships and if we don't my mom will come and bang us over the head.'

The father swiftly joins in.

'At the beginning of the day and in the middle of the day and at the end of the day, we are family. Nothing will divide us. That's our culture.'

There truly is sunshine at the heart of this relationship, but something sharp is hiding in the shadows. It is a clash of generations. You see it most clearly in the son; he guards his impatience closely, but it is there. When he was twelve, he joined the other members of his political dynasty to help get Bill Clinton elected. Now he has no time for the Clinton dynasty. The torch must be passed from one generation to another.

The bond between father and son is strong enough to survive their differences, but they are there nonetheless. Where the father insists that he is no hyphenated American, the son talks of discovering the hidden lesson of his ethnic identity while at college in Austin. 'I became more Hispanic than I had ever been because you rely on that culture to remind you of who you are, to give you a voice.'

The son means no disrespect to the father, but he is clearly trying to find an identity outside his father's shadow. He entered politics because he wanted to emulate his father's achievements, but he speaks with impatience about the need for new leadership, for a new politics. And as if to underline the point, he is the first to leave his chair by the water's edge.

His father is late for another interview and still has to dress for the parade later in the day. His aide, Louie, is now pointing at his watch, but the older man has one last thing to show his visitors. 'This area is famous for its citrus fruits,' he says, as he walks towards the grapefruit trees, alive with green and yellowy-pink. He asks Louie to go and get some plastic bags. He wants his visitors to take some fruit with them on their journey to Austin.

This veteran politician is happier now than he has been all morning. All broad smiles and talk of how much he loves south Texas. He insists we fill the bags with grapefruit. Each fruit is the size of a small football. (The next morning, one of the grapefruit will be taken from the bag, the skin peeled back and the rose-coloured fruit torn in in half. The juice will cascade like water all over the carpet of an Austin hotel room.)

Eddie Lucio Senior has lived a life of achievement. At the centre of his six acres, we stand by that grapefruit tree, basking in his happiness. He has reached his destination. It will soon be time for another generation to shoulder the burden.

—•—

On 4 March 2007, Barack Obama was still considered to be a long shot in the race for the White House, but he made a speech that day in Brown Chapel in Selma, Alabama, which deserves a place in history. It marks the moment when the Joshua Generation officially showed its hand.

Obama and Clinton had both travelled to city of Selma to mark the 42nd anniversary of Martin Luther King's march on Montgomery. In his speech, Obama described the leaders of the civil rights movement as leaders of the 'Moses generation':

> We are in the presence today of a lot of Moseses. We're in the presence today of giants whose shoulders we stand on, people who battled, not just on behalf of African-Americans but on behalf of all of America; that battled for America's soul, that shed blood, that endured taunts and torment and in some cases gave the full measure of their devotion.

Obama said that the Moses generation had left a lasting legacy for those who followed, particularly himself. But as the speech continued, it became clear that Obama had come to announce the arrival of a new generation as much as applaud another. He pointed out that Moses never crossed the river Jordan. God stopped him short of the the Promised Land. The Moses generation would wander in the desert until a new generation was born, and a new leader called Joshua took over.

> The previous generation, the Moses generation, pointed the way. They took us 90% of the way

97

there. We still got that 10% in order to cross over to
the other side. So the question, I guess, that I have
today is: what's called of us in this Joshua
generation? What do we do in order to fulfill that
legacy; to fulfill the obligations and the debt that we
owe to those who allowed us to be here today?

In that speech, Barack Obama was offering a genuine insight
into the seeds of the next American reinvention. The Joshua
generation does exist and it fits neatly into the cycle of
generational conflict that shapes American history. It is a
process that historians Neil Howe and William Strauss describe
as the 'the intersections of the seasons of life with the seasons
of time'.

Howe and Strauss are pioneers of the study of generational
struggle. To try to understand the United States, they say,
without paying attention to the rivalry of generations 'is like
trying to understand the movement of the oceans by looking at
the breaking waves while ignoring the tide'. They believe that
every 80 years or so, a Joshua generation appears in America. It
is a 'civic' generation which sets out to rebuild after the excesses
of an 'idealist' generation. Its purpose is to restore balance to a
society that has lost its way, to defuse the fervour and conflict the
'idealists' had provoked.

At key moments in American history, the rise of this
generation coincides with a political realignment, which comes
roughly every 40 years. Just as history moves between 'civic' and
'idealist' generations, political power tends to switch every four
decades between liberals (pushing the public dimension of
politics) and conservatives (emphasising the freedom of the
individual). To put that in a context with which we are already
familiar, American politics is a pendulum swinging between
Frontier and Ritual. The last great realignment began with
Richard Nixon's victory in 1968; Republicans went on to win

most of the presidential elections that followed and made Sunbelt conservatism the dominant philosophy of an era.

You don't have to be a genius to work out that if you add 40 years to 1968 you get 2008. The timeline of history suggests that it is time for a realignment. But what about a broader generational transformation? Have we reached that once-in-a-lifetime junction of history? There are certainly signs of a civic revival in the most dynamic parts of America, but before we go jumping to any conclusions, let us take a closer look at the Joshua generation.

The first important thing to know about the Joshua generation is that its biggest component is the Millennial generation (a name chosen by the Millennials themselves in a national survey). There is some disagreement about when they were born: some say as early as 1978; others say 1982. Either way, they are the largest generation in American history, with anything between 80 and 100 million members. This is the generation Eddie Lucio III speaks for.

To understand what makes the Millennials tick, you have to understand the generations that preceded them. There is Generation X, a neglected group, full of alienation and ironic detachment, now slouching towards middle age. They live in the shadow of the generation that sets the pace of American life: the rapidly ageing Baby Boomers, born in the years after World War II. This is Senator Eddie Lucio Jr's generation.

If you accept the Strauss and Howe definition, the Boomers are the 'idealist' generation who were 'reared in an indulgent manner and are driven throughout their lives by their deeply held values'. They are prepared to fight for their ideals, even if that means permanent conflict. They are in touch with their inner selves and place a high premium on self-awareness and individual achievement. The Boomers were the Moses generation who struggled to change the world, but eventually were sucked into three decades of 'culture war' in which liberal notions of personal freedom were pitted against the (often more dominant) conservative version.

By contrast, the civic generation are 'reared in a highly protected manner so that an orientation to societal challenges, problem-solving, and institution-building marks their adult lives'. They are team-orientated, focussed on results and have little desire to contemplate their 'inner life'. If they are going to rebel against anything, it is the Boomer notion of rebellion. As Strauss and Howe put it: 'It's more correct to call Millennials anti-Boomers, history's correctives for the mistakes they perceive that their parents are making.'

Plenty of American writers are falling in love with the Millennial generation, comparing them to the last 'civic' generation in American politics: the G.I. generation or 'Greatest generation', which elected Franklin Delano Roosevelt, backed the liberal vision of his 'New Deal', won World War II and then came back to build the suburbs.

Their biggest fans see in the Millennials 'a remoralising of American society', to quote Francis Fukuyama. I get the sense that many of these Millennial enthusiasts are actually parents of Millennial kids who believe their model offspring reflect well on their parenting skills. The Millennials are certainly the most looked-after kids in American history. One 2005 study showed that 9,000 books on self-esteem in children were written during the 1980s and 1990s, just as Millennials were being raised. By comparison, just 500 books on these topics were written in the 1970s when the poor GenXers wandered about aimlessly in search of adult supervision. Some have suggested that the Millennial era can really be traced to the moment when the first 'Baby on Board' sticker was placed on a minivan or the first bicycle helmet was placed on a reluctant kid's head.

The principal by-product of all that care and attention is a remarkable confidence. As they come of age, Millennials do share the public doubts of other generations. In a poll taken in

June 2007, 70 per cent said that their nation was on wrong track. But other surveys show that the Millennials are hugely optimistic about their own lives, about their potential to move ahead in life and about the likelihood of doing better than previous generations. They also have an enormous faith in their own ability to create change. In that 2007 survey, 77 per cent said that their votes would have a great bearing on who the next president is.

As well as having faith in themselves, the Millennials have faith in technology; it is their first language. All they know about communication they learned from MySpace, iPod, Napster, Wii, Ti-Vo, Facebook and YouTube. Nobody understands the tools of the American reinvention better than they do. One poll in 2006 found that 18- to 25-year-olds spend an average of 21.3 hours per week online. Another survey in 2007 found that 80 per cent of Millennials over the age of 14 had created a personal profile on at least one of the social networking sites and three-quarters said that they updated their page every week.

Once again, what is important here is the group. The technology the Millennials favour connects them with a wider world rather than consigning them to an empty room. Their group orientation points them to socially productive behaviour like joining and volunteering. A survey of American college campuses in 2005 showed that 83 per cent of those entering their first year had volunteered at least once in the previous year and 71 per cent said they volunteered on a weekly basis.

All the evidence suggest that the Millennials have faith in rules. They use fewer drugs, have less pre-marital sex and break the law less than previous generations. There were 3 million acts of teenage crime in America 1993 just as Generation X was slipping into its slow, self-destructive spiral. In 2003, there were just 300,000 (and remember, there are far more Millennials than GenXers, so the figures underestimate the relative fall in criminality).

101

What is remarkable about all this social goodness is that it emerges out of the suburban sprawl which some analysts predicted would bring America to its knees. The Millennials have bucked almost every trend established by the GenXers and the Boomers except one: their drift to the boomburbs. We know that, by 2000, 50 per cent of Americans lived in suburbs, and there is every sign that their Millennial kids will continue to circulate within the boomburb universe, even if they move to a different part of it.

If you need further proof of this trend, just talk to the jewellers. In 2007, the International Diamond Exchange (IDEX) urged the jewellery industry to follow the Millennials as they migrated ever deeper into the Sunbelt (market research shows they share the Baby Boomers' love of bling). IDEX cited statistics from the US Department of Commerce which showed that nine of the top ten growth markets for Millennials are in Sunbelt states; they are expected to increase their consumption by 40 per cent in Arizona and 35 per cent in Nevada. All this against an average national growth in consumer markets of five per cent.

These trends will be hard to believe if you still see migrants to the Sunbelt suburbs as older, white, working-class refugees fleeing the noisy, multicolour reality of modern America. That perception is no longer valid. The Sunbelt is getting younger, more diverse and more industrious. It is also more educated. Between 1995 and 2000, the increase in the number of people with college degrees in Phoenix was greater than in any other city in the United States bar Atlanta. Las Vegas, too, saw its graduate population rise by over 20 per cent in the late 1990s. Demographers are now talking of 'Bright Flight', with booming job markets on the Sunbelt Frontier drawing in a flood of well-educated professionals.

At some point in the last twenty years, the dynamo of American capitalism moved out of the big cities. In the 1990s, three-quarters of all new office space was created in the suburbs, and job growth there was three times higher than in the downtowns. Again, the most intense growth was felt along the Sunbelt Frontier, from northern California to the 'Silicon Hills' in Austin, Texas, the headquarters for computer giant Dell and an increasingly important centre for high-tech research.

As industry migrates, so too do the Millennials, and what comes with them are the trappings of a cosmopolitan community. As they put down roots, the Millennials demanding the perks of big-city living in sprawling suburbs or old frontier towns. As the writer Joel Kotkin puts it: 'Espresso and art follow good jobs, not the other way around.'

In certain parts of the Sunbelt, you certainly have to look for the cosmopolitan presence amid the generic clutter, and that makes the discovery all the more fulfiling. One of the genuine pleasures of a journey through the Southwest is stumbling across well-adjusted Millennials in cool little pockets of Sunbelt bohemia. Some Southwestern towns have the added attraction of being college towns. That's where you meet the Joshua generation at its grittiest, hairiest best (my personal recommendations are weeknight music in the open-air courtyard of Emos in Austin, or drinks and dinner at John Dillinger's last hideout, the Congress Hotel in Tucson).

Drive out into the desert and you will eventually run into one of a growing number of 'New West' communities, transformed from hardy frontier outposts into hotbeds of cool. Many were established by old hippies and Boomers searching for themselves but they have swollen with the flow of incoming Millennials. Take the town of Bisbee in southern Arizona: once a violent, frontier copper camp, it is now a hip artists' colony with a distinctly liberal feel about it (the stickers on the wall at St. Elmo's bar say 'Pray for a secular state' and 'Impeach Bush').

Even in the sprawling boomburb constellation that surrounds Phoenix you can find superficial reflections of the range of Millennial tastes: dive bars in Mesa, sushi in Gilbert,

Thai in Chandler, Goth music downtown. In Scottsdale on any given Friday you can watch the beautiful Millennials parade into the bar at the uber-chic Mondrian Hotel or watch them play high school football just up the road.

H.G. Wells predicted that the city of the future would be transformed from places of business into a 'a great gallery of shops and places of concourse and rendezvous'. Boomburbs are not necessarily what he had in mind, but there is an awful lot of rendezvous-ing going on among the Sunbelt Millennials. Perhaps the best guide to the soul of a modern American city or suburb is the listings on Meetup.com, which connects people with like-minded clubs and groups in their areas.

If you look up listings for Gilbert, for example, you see plenty of self-realised Boomers at play in groups such as East Valley Psychics (63 members), the Wild Outdoors Christian Fellowship (102 members) and the Adults 'Swingers Lifestyle' Group (it has only three members though, which seems to defeat the purpose). But there is a distinct Millennial presence among the hundreds of people signed up to groups for Single Friends, Childfree Friends, Shooting Pool, Ultimate Frisbee, and Dungeons and Dragons.

Extend the search to the wider Valley of the Sun, which includes Phoenix and its boomburbs, and things get even more interesting. You might well detect a Millennial backlash against Boomer spirituality in the 300-member strong Phoenix Witches Meetup Group, the Phoenix Werewolf Meetup Group (21 members) and the Atheist Anti-Church Fellowship (33 members). It is hard to decide what to think about the Phoenix Procrastinators Meetup (10 members). And as for the 19 members of Wonderbreath, your guess is as good as mine. But there is just no doubt about which generation is being served by the Arizona Karaoke Community, Phoenix New In Town Girls Night Out, 20s and 30s Social Meetup and In Our 20s & New

To Phoenix. When you add them together, these groups have more than 1,000 members.

Now we have met the Millennials in their natural habitat. We know they like each others' company, and don't like conflict. They sound like nice, polite young people, but nothing yet suggests they hold a candle to the G.I. generation; the invention of Facebook hardly ranks up there with the defeat of Nazi Germany.

Really.

How much faith can you have in a generation that would rather socialise than start a revolution?

5.
Orangewood – No Me without Us

'Happiness,' says the girl with the blonde hair and a cute, button nose.

'Very good,' says her teacher, Randy Tucker.

His class are discussing the declaration of independence and its promise of life, liberty and the pursuit of … what, class?

Happiness.

Very good.

'Did the Declaration of Independence tell us we are guaranteed to be happy?'

The answer comes in a hesitant chorus.

'No.'

'If it doesn't guarantee us the right to be happy, it guarantees us the right to … what?'

Randy points to another girl, this time with long brown hair and eyes that speak of wisdom beyond her years.

'We have the right to be happy, but it doesn't always mean we are going to be happy. It means we have the right to pru … pursue our dreams.'

Randy expresses particular satisfaction with this answer, rolling his 'r's in appreciation.

'Verrrry good,'

Randy Tucker is a tall well-built man with a shaven head. When he was younger, he served in the US Marines. There is a photograph of him in uniform at the back of the classroom. He is ruggedly handsome and young behind the glass frame, square-jawed, and emotionless. It is the kind of picture you have seen before, a thousand times, next to a headline about American casualties in Iraq. But this portrait is surrounded by life and energy.

Randy teaches the older children at Orangewood Elementary School, which nestles in one of the older, inner suburbs of Phoenix. Their classroom is plastered with images drawn from America's civic fables and unifying struggles. On the wall at the back is a vivid, painted rendition of the iconic image of the Marines raising the flag on Iwo Jima. The slogan on the poster reads: 'Now all together.' At the front of the classroom, to the left of the whiteboard, is the Stars and Stripes, hanging at a 45-degree angle.

Randy's students should be comfortable with the explicit patriotism on display in this classroom; after all, this is the tail end of the Millennial generation. The burden of history sits comfortably on these young shoulders. They see nothing to fear in values, traditions and conventional wisdom.

Which is fine, up to a point. But there is a niggling doubt in the minds of some American elders about what the Millennials bring to the table. They worry about an apparent absence of scepticism and critical thinking. They know that this is a civic generation, but they worry that it is also a cipher generation which will embrace the American ideal without necessarily adding to it.

In a previous class, Randy Tucker had set his class a challenge. He had asked them to cast ballots for their favourite freedom, sort of like America's Greatest Hits. As you might expect from a generation that thrives on communication, the number one freedom was freedom of speech.

'Number two,' Randy announces, 'is freedom to choose how you dress.'

Randy doesn't judge, but from his words you can tell he is a little perplexed.

'Is that what the founding fathers had in mind?' He asks this rhetorically, but then makes a genuine inquiry: 'Why is it important to you?'

'I don't want to wear something ugly,' says one girl, confidently.

'It's important to give me personality,' says one of the boys.

With the number three freedom, we are back on safer ground; the children have voted for 'the ability to choose our own leaders'. Then we return to the unexpected. At number four in the freedom hit parade is the 'ability to choose who we will marry'. Randy is gently sceptical.

'I can guarantee George Washington and Thomas Jefferson didn't have that in mind.'

As well as freedom to marry at will, freedom of religion makes it in to the top five, reminding us of the uncommon morality of American youngsters. Freedom to travel without documents is at number six, speaking of their growing wanderlust.

'How many have travelled outside of Arizona?' Randy asks and the hands shoot up.

'All of us, good. Now, what freedom would you sacrifice for?'

It's a tough question which you would never ask of a group of pre-teen children back in Ireland. Of course, there is a completely different context for sacrifice in the United States.

'Remember some of our men and women are sacrificing for our freedom in what two countries?'

'Baghdad,' says a young male voice.

'Yes, but what country?'

'Iraq,' replies the chorus.

'And what other country?'

'Iran,' a boy offers.

'No, hopefully not Iran,' says Randy, and you can hear the little chuckle in his voice. 'Begins with an "A".'

'Afghanistan,' comes a near-unanimous response.

'So, what freedom would you sacrifice for?'

In quick succession, equal rights and religion are mentioned.

'Any other freedoms you'd be willing to sacrifice for?'

Freedom of speech.

Again, with the talking …

You can't help but be charmed by those kids, with their determination to speak and dress and marry as they like. But it is Randy Tucker's empathy and commitment which really leave an imprint. His gentle encouragement is such a contrast to the aggressive coaching you often see directed at American kids. There is positive energy in that class but no over-inflated praise. And there is talk of obligations as well as rights, duty as much as entitlement.

This is the American way, but not always the Millennial way.

—•—

The Millenials are the offspring of 'the era of the worthy child', which was a wider backlash against the moral panic, pessimism and alienation which took a firm grip of America in the late 1970s. Parents set out to raise an 'antidote generation' by banishing bad habits and filling their kids' lives with purpose and positive energy. Studies show that the amount of time kids under the age of 12 spent watching television declined in the 1980s and 90s by almost a quarter, and the amount of sport they played went up by roughly the same margin.

The Millennials certainly never wanted for active encouragement and affirmation, but some question the impact of that constant praise. Psychology professor Jean Twenge has big concerns about how the Millennials were raised, as you will probably glean from the title of her 2007 book, *Generation Me: Why Today's Young Americans Are More Confident, Assertive, Entitled — and More Miserable than Ever Before.*

'They were raised by "helicopter" parents,' says Twenge, 'who constantly hovered over them – providing unending praise, support and, perhaps, unrealistic expectations that the world was their oyster.'

There is a growing body of evidence to support that view. One financial services company surveyed American high school kids in 2006 and found that 61 per cent expect to become millionaires in their 40s or younger.

Professor Twenge carried out a survey of more than 16,000 college students which applied a 'standardized narcissistic personality inventory', asking for responses to such questions as 'I think I am a special person.' The survey found that students in 2006 were 30 per cent more narcissistic than the average student in 1982.

As the Millennials enter the workplace employers feel pressure to keep up with 'praise inflation'. Some top corporations bring in consultants to teach managers how to compliment employees with emails, prizes, 'Celebration Voice Mailboxes' and a range of public displays of appreciation. One Texas company called Scooter Store Inc. has a staff 'celebrations assistant' who throws twenty-five pounds of confetti at employees each week and passes out 100 to 500 celebratory helium balloons.

If employers do need to chastise their Millennial workers, they have to be very careful. 'You do have to speak to them a little bit like a therapist on television might speak to a patient,' says trend-watcher Marian Salzman of advertising agency J. Walter Thompson. 'You can't be harsh. You can't really ask them to live and breathe the company, because they're living and breathing themselves – and that keeps them very busy.'

Another increasingly common complaint about young Americans is that they have become intellectually lazy, turning their back on knowledge which is not absolutely vital to material success. Consider a 2006 *National Geographic* poll that found nearly half of 18- to 24-year-olds don't think it is necessary or important to know where countries in the news are located.

Author Jeff Gordiner is particularly tough on the Millennials in his book *X Saves the World*, which is a spirited defence of his own GenX cohort. He cites the classic movie version of *Willie Wonka and the Chocolate Factory* as an allegory for our times. The hero is Charlie Bucket, the grounded kid who doesn't sell out (representing Generation X), and the villain, Veruca Salt. Years later, her cry of 'I want it now' will become, according to Gordiner, 'nothing less than a mission statement for the Millennials' .

Gordiner says that this generation of Veruca Salts are so fixated on brands, celebrities and stuff that they won't read anything longer than a caption on a photograph. 'Because literacy leads to self reflection and critical thinking, and self reflection and critical thinking open the door to doubt and scepticism, and stuff like that just gets in the way when you're trying to get ahead, and *OMG did you see how fat Britney looks these days?!?!?*

By now, we have a pretty long list of indictments against young Americans: they are narcissistic, naive, shallow, ignorant and easily manipulated. There is one last complaint on the charge sheet: apathy. The critics says Millennials have no interest in being the agents of change who would transform America.

Just look at their attitude to the Iraq war. Young Americans oppose the war by a big majority, but they have not followed through with the kind of mass action which characterised the Vietnam era. Their popular culture doesn't reflect the sound of protest the same way the music of the sixties did. 'Let's face it,' said *Rolling Stone* senior editor David Fricke, 'people are distracted … they spend more time watching "American Idol" than they do voting in the last couple of elections.'

So much of what the sceptics say sounds credible. But something is not quite right. The dark portrait of the Millennial bears an uncanny resemblance to the shallow view of America we started out with. It is the narrow perspective of a green-eyed voyeur peering through the keyhole with a mixture of revulsion and fascination.

—•—

The common thread linking the harshest criticism of the Millennials is a failure of imagination. As the critics prod and poke young Americans, they are mesmerised by the surface details and remain oblivious to the altered consciousness which lurks inside. The Millennials don't just play by different rules; they play a different game, and the greatest game-changing force is technology.

Every aspect of youth culture is different in the digital age. This is sometimes portrayed as a man-made revolution, but it makes more sense to see it as an organic process, a cascading mutation which improves with each quickening stage of evolution. You only have to consider the impact of this evolutionary leap on music to see what impact it is having on the Joshua generation.

The advent of the MP3 and the iPod, and the online music stores which supply them, has shattered old certainties. Writer Chris Anderson argues in his book *The Long Tail* that the era of the blockbuster is over. People have moved away from the top of the supply chain, where a small number of big hits are sold, towards a 'long tail', where they will find niche music that best reflects their personalities. In the past, 20 per cent of the music has made 80 per cent of the money, but now each piece of music has a market. Anderson reported that every one of the one million musical tracks on iTunes has sold at least once (and the number of tracks has at least doubled since he wrote his book).

In the past, people listened to the same music on the same radio stations and bought their music from a chain of record shops. 'Back in the pre-digital era,' says Professor Robert

Thompson of Syracuse University, 'we all ate from the same culture trough, whether you like it or not.' (That is part of the reason that 60s' protest music had such power; it was the soundtrack to everyone's lives.)

Musical tastes were often limited by where you lived because it took real effort to physically acquire music outside the mainstream. Think of that inquisitive suburban teenager making a weekly pilgrimage to the nearest town in the hope that the dingy basement record shop might have some rarity in stock.

In contrast, in the digital era, you are never more than a couple of keystrokes away from the obscure and exotic sound. The dingy basement record shop in Seattle or SoHo is now open for business in Surprise or Gilbert. The physical barriers between suburbia and bohemia are removed, at least in the online music library.

Digital music not only encourages curiosity, it rewards it, thanks to those unknowable algorithms at the heart of digital technology. With each step you take inside the online music store, a hidden high-tech hand leads you closer to your very own musical nirvana. The ghost in the machine is actually your own inner voice saying, 'try it, you might like it'. Those who have followed this journey find that their comfort zones are expanded to an extent not easily described. 'As they wander farther from the beaten path,' observes Chris Anderson, 'they discover their tastes are not as mainstream as they thought.'

Hidden depths are exposed as soon as the individual is liberated from the dictatorship of other people's choices. Sophistication is no longer rationed out in hip neighbouroods of big cities. Quality is no longer determined by an elite band of cultural gate-keepers. Popularity is no longer dictated by faceless brand managers. It doesn't take a computer scientist to see how this might alter a generation's expectations of the society they live in.

Even 'old media' moguls like Rupert Murdoch see the writing on the wall. 'Young people don't want to rely on a God-like figure from above to tell them what's important,' Murdoch said in 2005. 'They want control over their media, instead of being controlled by it.'

Of course, change brings risks. Like the inflated praise heaped on the Millennials, the hyper-individualistic ethic of the digital age threatens objective standards of quality. Critics make the valid point that much of what is offered along that 'long tail' offers no cultural nutrition. This view is best expressed in an aphorism known as Sturgeon's Revelation: '90 per cent of everything is crap.'

If you are near a laptop, put the book down for a moment and call up the YouTube home page. At the time of writing, the top featured video showed a fast-talking puppet performing a fairytale called the 'Frog Princess'. Below that was a two-minute clip illustrating the visual effects of sound waves on a loud-speaker. Other videos included the continuing adventures of Gregory Shitcock ('the smartest private detective in the world'), something entitled 'Robo-Jew Versus the Giant Nazi Woman' and snippets from a new TV series called *The 'Bu* about 'young, sexy people that live in Malibu'.

If you stop right there, at that opening page of YouTube (as many critics seem to do), you will find plenty of reasons to mourn the passing of civilisation, but type a few key words into the YouTube search engine that reflect your definition of high culture – say 'classical music'. If you did that on the day these words were written, you would have been transported in seconds to a performance of Prokofiev's Quartet No. 2, Opus 92, played by the Minneapolis-based Artarian String Quartet. Admittedly, the second most popular video in this category featured talk-show host Craig Anderson telling a joke about demented squirrels at a classical music concert, but you get the point.

New media platforms like YouTube give us the tools to bypass the great wall of crud and white noise in the blink of an eye. Forget the 90 per cent of crap; the 10 per cent of quality has never been so accessible. Because there has been an exponential growth in the volume of online material to choose from, that 10 per cent offers so much more than the critics give it credit for.

The digital age hasn't just expanded choice, it has turned consumers into producers. Ordinary people now have access to technology that used to be reserved for the media professionals. They are using it to create a 'mash-up' culture in which images of life are recorded and downloaded and then broken up into bits and pieces, edited, remixed, infused with personality and put back on a website like YouTube for all to see.

The great attraction of the mash-up culture is that each individual is guaranteed a corner of cyber-space in which they will excel. Since there is a market for every product, you will never fail to draw an audience. In a virtual world, the Millennial generation will never fall short.

It is also much easier to be an innovator in this environment because once you share your new idea, others make it work. You don't seem to need the same level of intense, exhausting focus to create change. The founder of Meetup, Scott Heiferman, was inspired to make a difference after reading Robert Putnam's *Bowling Alone*, which revealed the decline of community in the United States. 'Although the big joke,' he later admitted, 'is that I never actually read the whole thing. I didn't have the attention span.'

The word 'viral' has come to be associated with the process of online creation and that perfectly captures the social element of the process. The work of any one individual becomes valuable when it contaminates an audience, when it finds a host crowd in which to mutate and spread. On social networking sites like MySpace and Facebook, each individual life gathers meaning and significance as it is shared with friends and exposed to strangers. This central assumption of the digital age is now the philosophy of a generation: there is no 'me' without 'us'.

The most remarkable meeting point of individual and community is the online encyclopaedia, Wikipedia, which as of April 2008 offered 10 million articles in 253 languages to 683 million visitors every year. All articles are collaboratively written by a worldwide team of volunteers and edited by anyone with access to the Internet. Wikipedia works on the basis of consensus and civic trust; people believe it or else they wouldn't visit it in such huge numbers.

There is a strong argument that Wikipedia is open to bias, manipulation and vandalism, although one contested study found that information on Wikipedia was at least as accurate as conventional encyclopaedias. But an undoubted advantage is that it is 'a living community rather than a static reference work'. Mistakes tend to get corrected and new information gets added as it becomes available.

Wikipedia also acts as a vital clearing house for information. The best recent example came in April 2007 when a young gunman went on a killing spree on the campus of Virginia Tech. More than 2,000 Wikipedia editors, some working as far away as Finland, began filtering information as it became available. Their constantly evolving article eventually had more than 140 footnotes, as well as profiles of the killer, Seung-Hui Cho, and a timeline of the attacks. More than 750,000 visited the article in its first two days, an average of four visits a second, and it was highly rated as a reference tool, even by local newspapers.

Natalie Erin Martin is a 23-year-old student from Ohio and one of the editors who worked on the Virginia Tech article. She gave a remarkable insight into the workings of Wikipedia to the *New York Times*. 'People seem to self-assign,' she said. 'A lot of people went, "Oh, my God! This happened. It's going to be historic. I better make sure this isn't a problem." It has all been out of a sense of personal responsibility.'

It is often said that the problem with Wikipedia is that it only works in practice; it is impossible to understand in theory. The same can be said of the Joshua generation. Forget about Veruca Salt and her screams of 'I want it now'. Keep in mind Natalie Erin Martin and her eternal Millennial truth: 'People seem to self-assign.'

It's also worth remembering that Wikipedia is a living organism, and so is this American reinvention. That is not simply a metaphor. The image exists in a physical form on YouTube, where you can find an extraordinary video clip showing a time-lapse recording of that Virginia Tech article in its first 12 hours. The article practically becomes a biological entity, growing and contracting in rhythmic spurts, gaining definition, detail, substance and clarity, mimicking the earliest stages of life, growing bigger and more consequential.

The Millennials are the first generation of Americans to be raised inside the bio-sphere of the digital age and to grow in time with the captivating rhythms of social technology. This doesn't mean that we should excuse their faults or ignore their narcissistic streak. But this generation has been endowed with a talent for reinvention and our perspective needs to be broad enough to accommodate that.

Here are a few positive generalisations: young Americans have wider horizons and broader tastes; they embrace change but strive for consensus; they are self-reliant but also social; they are individuals within a collective. They have balanced Frontier and Ritual.

These broad truths hint at a brighter future for America. But there are questions yet to be answered. Will the Millennials live up to their potential as a transformational generation? Will they change America as much as they have altered its culture?

—•—

9/11 defines the Millennials more than it does any other segment of society. It is the event which, according to William Strauss and Neil Howe, has set the them on their way to becoming a 'hero' generation.

In the beginning, the Millennials reacted to the attack on the Twin Towers with an outburst of hawkishness. They over-whelmingly backed military action in Afghanistan and Iraq. Some surveys of young people showed they were actually more supportive of the use of force than other segments of society.

But there was a deeper impulse at work. The deepening partisan divisions of the 1990s (which climaxed with the Clinton impeachment saga) made them sensitive to the 'the ongoing fragmentation of American life', as Strauss and Howe put it. Even before 9/11, young Americans were drawn to institutions which brought unity and stability.

Perhaps the best way to understand the impact of 9/11 is as a hammer which embedded the 'civic' instinct in the Millennial psyche. It made them appreciate the federal government as a source of cohesion. In 2000, 36 per cent of college students said that they had faith in the government to do the right thing. In the wake of 9/11, 60 per cent gave the same answer. The Millennials are the most pro-government of all generations alive today.

Of course, this will upset the sceptics, who believe that the Millennials are far too respectful of authority. Worse still, these young Americans seem to shy away from a good political fight; three out of four off them say politics has become too partisan. Then there is their apathy; they are too busy messing with their Facebook profile or watching Britney's expanding waistline to care about who the next president is.

In truth, young Americans have been apathetic for decades. The number of 18- to 24-year-olds who voted fell from 52 per cent in 1972 to just 36 per cent in 2000. In a poll taken just before 9/11, only 28 per cent of college freshman said that keeping up with politics was important. America was, in the words of the National Commission on Civic Renewal, 'in danger of becoming a nation of spectators'.

And then along came the Joshua generation ready to perform their first great act of political reinvention. Forget the sceptics; they have misjudged young Americans. Millennials are well on their way to becoming the most politically engaged generation in modern American history.

9/11 sent a surge of civic patriotism through all segments of American society. But the heightened engagement faded relatively quickly, except among the Millennials. The survey of college students found interest in politics kept rising, year on year, to the extent that the researchers say that 'for today's freshmen, discussing politics is more prevalent than at any point in the past 41 years.' The Millennials weren't content to talk about politics, they have begun to act: in 2006, youth voter turnout reached a 20-year high.

The surge has continued into the 2008 presidential election season. Across all age groups, turnout has increased in the early primaries and caucuses, but as Robert Putnam points out, 'for twenty-somethings the rise has been truly phenomenal – turnout often three or four times greater than ever before measured.' A poll for the *Rock the Vote* group showed that youth turnout during the primary season all across America was up 109 per cent on the last election. The year 2008 could turn out to be what Putnam calls 'the coming-out party' of a new 'Greatest generation'.

In *Bowling Alone*, Putnam was worried about declining civic engagement. Now he is talking about a '9/11 generation', which embodies the civic spirit of the G.I. generation. Putnam says that the collapse of the Twin Towers was a life-changing moment for the 18-year-olds who cast their first vote in 2008. 'As we approached the presidential season of 2008,' Putnam says, 'Young Americans were, in effect, coiled for civic action, not because of their stage of life, but because of the lingering effects of the unifying national crisis they had experienced in their formative years.'

The sobering impact of 9/11 has coincided with the liberating potential of social technology, giving the Millennials both the means and the motive to shape politics. Young people are not content to watch; they want to take part. 'If broadcast media brought us broadcast politics,' says Jimbo Wales, the man who launched Wikipedia, 'then participatory media will bring us participatory politics'.

One in three young voters had visited a political website during the primary stages of the 2008 election and one in four MySpace users had a visited a candidate's page. Almost half said that they had talked or emailed about politics with friends.

The candidate who best understood this evolution in political activism was Barack Obama. His campaign had the benefit of insider information; among its early recruits was Chris Hughes, one of the developers of Facebook. From the beginning, the website my.barackobama.com was the backbone of the Obama campaign. It was more than a point of contact; it was a social networking hub from which you could download the makings of your own private Obama campaign, or just the latest accessories (the site offered 12 different Obama-themed ringtones). By the end of the primary season, my.barackobama.com had 750,000 active volunteers.

It is impossible to overstate the importance of the website in raising money. It sought out small monthly subscriptions but also offered volunteers the tools to set up private fund-raising operations, exploiting the great self-creating instinct of the digital age. Even before he had won the Democratic nomination, Obama had raised $200 million online, almost 10 times what Internet-savvy Howard Dean pulled in during his bid for the White House in 2004.

The amount was unprecedented, but so too was the absence of ethical baggage. Obama didn't need to soil himself with the usual tawdry fund-raisers; he didn't need to rely on corporate donations. During the month of February 2008, he raised $45 million without holding a single conventional fund-raising event. All told, 94 per cent of donations to Obama's campaign were $200 or less. The same could be said of just 13 per cent of donations to John McCain's campaign.

The Obama campaign did have its problems with the Internet, which mercilessly exposes politicians who are less than open and consistent. Barack Obama learned that lesson when his former pastor Reverend Jeremiah Wright ended up on YouTube 'God-Damning' America, and Obama stumbled and fumbled as he tried to detach himself.

But, overall, the Internet has been very good to Obama on many different levels. The success of his online campaign mirrored those pioneering Silicon Valley companies which created social technology. It sent a message to the Millennials and the architects of the digital age: I am one of you. 'Obama was the new, new thing,' said one Silicon Valley entrepreneur, 'and that is what we are all about here.'

Obama's campaign understood that the internet was more than just a campaign tool. In the digital age, politics also has a 'long tail'. A winning campaign can no longer rely on big-budget advertising and a generic message. It must build a new type of grass roots campaign with the potential to reach every niche. Soundbites on the national news become so much less important than the endorsement of the mayor of Oskaloosa, Iowa.

Barack Obama has also benefited from shifting political sympathies among Millennial voters. One study by the Pew Research Centre found that 48 per cent of 18- to 25-year-olds now identify with or lean toward the Democrats, while just 35 per cent plumps for the Republicans. That is a fairly stark reversal from the early 1990s, when 55 per cent of GenXers at that age backed the Republican Party.

Underpinning this drift toward the Democrats are growing liberal sentiments on some social issues among American young people. A clear majority of Millennials support gay marriage; according to a 2007 poll, an equally clear majority of older Americans opposed it. The message from the Joshua generation on this and other so-called wedge issues is: 'Get over it.'

Everything we have discovered about the Millennial generation suggests that they are a perfect fit with Barack Obama. Above all, Obama shares the Millennial's core mission: undo the damage wrought by the Boomers. Writing in his campaign book, *The Audacity of Hope*, he said that he wanted an end to 'the psychodrama of the Baby Boom generation – a tale rooted in old grudges and revenge plots hatched on a handful of college campuses long ago'.

However, on closer examination of the Millennial psyche, you see the problems for Obama in his match-up with John McCain. To begin with, McCain's anti-Boomer credentials were equally as strong as Obama's. He could put serious distance between himself and bitter, partisan bickering that emerged from the sixties. 'I wasn't there,' he said, referring to his own captivity in Vietnam, 'I was tied up at the time.' He is being touted as being from the best of the generations that preceded it, a return to an era of public service and personal responsibility.

McCain had long since broken with the 'culture warriors' in the Republican Party, but he spoke of patriotic themes which resonated with young Americans. They may have drifted towards the Democrats, but they are still very traditional when it comes to issues such as the stability of the family or the nation. In a study by advertising company J. Walter Thompson, 94 per cent of Millennials said that they respect monogamy and parenthood, while 84 per cent revere marriage and an equal number respect the military.

Millennials confound the traditional definition of liberal or conservative. They tend to live moral lives but are slow to judge others. They want the government to bring order, but appreciate the value of self-reliance. In politics, the Millennials are looking for the balance of Ritual and Frontier that they have found in social networking.

Whether or not they bring about a political realignment in 2008, they will be a force for change.

But change is such a modest goal for a generation overflowing with talent and ambition. The Joshua generation has the potential for so much more than that. But there are still those unresolved questions posed by Randy Tucker: What would the Millennials sacrifice for? What is the great challenge that will secure their place in history?

—•—

Morning has broken. The sky is clear. The sun is burning bright. So why do you feel like Dorothy, lost in the Emerald City?

You are standing in the north tower of a hotel shaped like a pyramid, looking out at a hotel shaped like a cartoon castle. It's blue and red turrets standing guard over the perpetual motion of Highway 15 which communes briefly with Las Vegas, collecting its automotive waste before returning to the Mojave Desert.

In the background, the television is tuned to the *Today* programme.

'I am Matt Lauer and I'm reporting from the town of Ilulissat, third-largest town in Greenland. The noise you hear in the background is the halibut-processing factory … '

NBC's flagship morning show has sent its hosts to the 'ends of the earth' to report on the impact of climate change. Matt Lauer is close to the North Pole, his colleague Ann Currie is near the South Pole and weatherman Al Roker is broadcasting from the Equator.

Back in studio, the reserve anchor is interviewing Chip Giller, the author of a new book called *Wake Up and Smell the Planet*. In four minutes, he gives seven hints on how to fight global warming, one person at a time. Among his suggestions are skipping meat once a week and ditching the car occasionally. Back in that Las Vegas hotel room, Chip is competing with the drone of Highway 15 and the siren song of the breakfast buffet.

Down in the restaurant, the waitress is an elegant lady in late middle-age with a strained look on her face. She wears a badge on her chest which advertises the hotel's topless cabaret. In the nearby bar, two young women dressed in colourful 50s-style cocktail dresses sit giggling at the bar as they polish off the remains of a bottle of something bubbly.

It is just shy of 9 a.m.

The distinguished Las Vegas historian Hal Rothman described his city as a 'liberation from the burden of sin'. It sticks in your mind as you stroll down the Strip past immigrant men advertising escort services, swarms of bachelorettes and rental car services offering Lamborghinis by the hour. Rothman suggests that Las Vegas is a refuge from the puritan instinct in American life, but what if it were also a window to a deeply embedded delusion?

If you time it right, you will arrive at the Bellagio Hotel just as the show is about to begin. All around the eight-acre replica of Lake Como, *Viva Las Vegas* seeps from unseen speakers and the fountains begin to bubble gently. Within seconds they explode high into the Vegas sky, obscuring the fake Eiffel Tower just across the water.

This city gets just four inches of rainfall every year – making it the driest urban area in America – but it has the highest rate of water consumption of any big US city. The mammoth hotels on the Strip are symbols of this shortfall, but they are not the cause; 70 per cent of the water used in southern Nevada comes out of water sprinklers, working desperately to stop suburban lawns from turning into sand.

Las Vegas is the adult fantasy which lurks in a shady corner of the American dream. But it is also a nice place to start a new life. In 2006, at the very peak of that Great Dispersal, a new resident was arriving in Vegas every six minutes and a new house was being built every 19 minutes. The fresh arrivals didn't come for the smorgasbord of excess along the Strip, but there was a touch of fantasy in the way they wanted to live.

In those sprawling Vegas suburbs, the pursuit of happiness is in danger of becoming a catastrophic environmental delusion. The United States will gain roughly 120 million people during the coming three decades and they will have to live somewhere. Just one in ten Americans wants to live in a city; half of them want to move to settle down in suburbs. The problem is that they keep flooding to suburbs that have been carved out of desert, like North Las Vegas, or its sister boomburb, Henderson.

Under the scorching sun, the new arrivals lay a carpet of concrete and asphalt, creating what scientists call 'urban heat islands' which send temperatures soaring to record-breaking heights. People put up with the heat because they have air-conditioning, but to keep the air cool, they need to use enormous amounts of energy. According to one independent energy watchdog, air-conditioning in the US now accounts for eight per cent of the world's total electricity supply.

More energy is needed to power bigger houses. Americans now occupy about 20 per cent more developed land per capita than they did twenty years ago. Public transport has never been a feature of these desert boomburbs, so everything revolves around the private car. Since 1980, the number of miles driven by Americans has increased three times faster than the number of people. The US Department of Energy expects this trend to continue; between now and 2030, the amount of driving is due to increase more than twice as much as the American population, unless something changes.

The American dream has never been lived on this scale, and it is impossible to find any scenario in which it can continue in this form. This turbo-charged pursuit of happiness is a relic of a different time, when oil was plentiful and cheap, when reservoirs were full and when climate change was science fiction. The Sunbelt boomburbs tell us that the American dream must reinvent itself, or face a potentially lethal collision with environmental reality.

The Book of Ecclesiastes says: 'One generation passeth away, and another generation cometh; but the earth abideth forever.' The Millennials may be the first generation not to have that certainty. America's looming environmental crisis is their defining challenge, the first great test of a potential 'hero' generation.

When asked to name the biggest problem their generation will need to tackle over the next 20 years, about 18 per cent of Millennials say the environment. That is almost twice as many as said terrorism. In the same opinion poll, 47 per cent said that candidates in the 2008 election should be talking more about the environment.

Young Americans are also beginning to apply themselves to environmental issues in a uniquely Millennial way, stressing autonomous, self-creating action, a sort of 'mash-up' political culture. A perfect example is the work of a California teenager called Taylor Francis, who became an environmental activist after watching Al Gore's hugely successful documentary *An Inconvenient Truth*. He flew to Nashville to be trained by Gore himself as a global warming educator working with a non-profit group called the Climate Project. So far, he has given his presentation to nearly 10,000 people, mostly high school students. At the ripe old age of 16, he travelled to China to spread the word among young people there.

The Millennial ethos of innovation, personal responsibility and faith in rules is beginning to make its mark on the Sunbelt. Out in those Las Vegas suburbs, new housing developments are being fitted with water conservation and energy-saving innovations, while those wasteful lawns are being ripped up and replanted with desert foliage, saving huge amounts of water. Las Vegas even has 'water police', who enforce strict water-rationing codes and impose heavy fines on rule-breakers.

The change in Millennial tastes is also promoting a trend towards sustainable development. The buzz-phrases among boomburb planners are 'New Urbanist neighbourhoods' (with more walking and cycling), 'transit-oriented development' (building around public transport hubs) and outdoor 'lifestyle centres' (to replace the traditional shopping mall).

In the age of the long tail, consumers are moving away from the heavily promoted, petrol-guzzling mega-cars. Hummer sales plummeted by 30 per cent in the first three months of 2008, while sales of the fuel-efficient hybrid, the Toyota Prius, rose by 54 per cent in 2007.

The sceptic could argue that this trend away from big, wasteful cars has been triggered by soaring fuel costs rather than a flowering 'green' consciouness, but does it really matter? The reality is that Americans now have a powerful economic incentive to change their ways and there are early, dramatic signs that they are doing just that. In March 2008, as prices at the petrol pump spiralled to record highs, Americans drove 11 billion fewer miles than in the same month in 2007. This was the biggest monthly fall in driving in the United States since records began in 1942.

Perhaps the pessimists have got it wrong. Maybe something really is happening in America. The country's most important local politicians certainly seem to think so. Governor Arnold Schwarzenegger has committed California to cutting carbon emissions by 25 per cent before 2020. New York is replacing its entire fleet of 13,000 yellow cabs with environmentally friendly hybrid cars. Austin is encouraging the use of solar panels in new houses, and Chicago has planted thousands of trees to cool 'urban heat islands'. They are even building a light rail system in Phoenix.

All this neatly serves the Millennials' preference for autonomous action within a social setting and their belief in the redeeming power of technology. But those who really know the scale of the impending crisis, and the distance America must make up, say that individual solutions and faith in technology will not be enough. With just a hint of condescension, the *New York Times* columnist Tom Friedman has warned the Joshua generation that they will need more than a digital sensibility to solve climate change: 'Martin Luther King and Bobby Kennedy didn't change the world by asking people to join their Facebook crusades or to download their platforms. Virtual politics is just that — virtual.'

Some Millennials get the message, including the 6,000 college students who gathered for the Power Shift summit in Washington in 2007 to call for the 80 per cent cut in carbon emissions, or the young activists of the nationwide Step It Up campaign, trying to force global warming to the top of the national political agenda.

But there are signs that many Millennials have not yet woken up to the scale of the collective test they now face. That poll which showed that one in five young Americans see the environment as the big challenge also showed it was not their number one concern. One in three picked economic difficulties as the defining challenge of the next twenty years.

We are back to the question Randy Tucker posed in that classroom: what would you sacrifice for? Even those who have captured the hearts of young Americans worry about the Millennials' apparent unwillingness to suffer for a cause greater than their own interest. 'I worry sometimes that the Joshua generation in its success forgets where it came from,' said Barack Obama during that speech in Selma. 'Thinks it doesn't have to make as many sacrifices. Thinks that the very height of ambition is to make as much money as you can.'

The underlying doubt here is whether the Millennials can

master the kind of change that involves pain and hardship. After all, they have been raised in a time of plenty, with an abundance of praise and a surplus of hope. Nothing has prepared them for the unique problems ahead, or for the fear that still shapes the lives of millions of Americans.

6.
Avalon – We Shall Overwhelm

Hollywood is unsentimental about its own history, but luckily the owners of the Avalon nightclub realised the commercial value of its past when they bought the property a few years ago. Instead of knocking down this old landmark a block from Hollywood and Vine, they revived old memories. Today, the history of the Avalon is one of the building's distinct selling points.

Before it was the Avalon, it was the Hollywood Palace and before that it was the Jerry Lewis Theatre, and before that, the El Capitan, and way back in the beginning it was the Hollywood Playhouse. For over three-quarters of a century, the venue has hosted everyone who ever mattered in the world of music and television, from Lucille Ball to the The Beastie Boys. It has staged plays by Henrik Ibsen, and a live TV performance of *The Muppet Show*. The Beatles played here in the 1960s, The Clash in the 1980s and Nirvana in the 1990s. Through all its incarnations, the Avalon has been a mirror to the evolution of the American soul.

It has even played a part in the evolution of American politics. In 1952, Richard Nixon delivered his famous 'Checkers' speech from the building. He spoke to millions of television viewers from a set designed to look like the front room of his home. Bill Clinton also came here in 1992 to announce one of the classic fudges of his political career, the 'Don't ask, don't tell' policy towards gays in the military. It was fitting, then, that the Barack Obama campaign in California chose the Avalon as the venue for its election night rally on Super Tuesday.

From the outside, the Avalon looks like an old Spanish mansion, with ornate carved columns rising alongside the imposing arched window which dominates the sandstone façade. But you are in Hollywood. A young man called Yosi is guarding the velvet rope with a clipboard in his hand and a fuzzy red beard keeping his face warm on this chilly February night. His body is a patchwork of perforations and tattoos all the way from his army surplus cap to his cycling shoes. 'Media?' he asks. 'Right this way.' The rope is uncoupled and Yosi motions to the club's vaulted, brightly lit entrance.

It's still a full hour before the polls are set to close on the West Coast, but results are already pouring out of the other 22 states holding primaries and caucuses that day. A line has formed outside the Avalon. The assembled faces look like one of those slick multi-racial advertisements for designer clothes or deodorant. White and brown, dreadlocked and blonde. The two women at the head of queue are wearing Mardi Gras beads and hats. An African-American man with a shaved head is wearing a T-shirt with Obama's image on the front under the words: 'He's black and I'm proud'.

The main hall inside holds 1,500 people and takes forever to fill up. The bulk of the crowd hang to the back, as if intimidated by the three giant TV screens broadcasting live coverage of the unfolding results. Bad news from New Jersey and Massachusetts. Good news in Missouri and Connecticut. But the crowd seems strangely detached from the wave of results that is surging forth. From the media enclosure up in the stalls, it appears that the people below seem more interested in themselves. And for good reason.

This crowd is a swelling constellation of race, ethnicity and fashion. Nobody seems to be older than thirty-five. There isn't an ugly person in the room (except up here among the hacks).

The drink is flowing liberally. There seems to be an edgy, flirtatious vibe in certain parts of the room. Somebody is going to do something quick.

'Yes we can. Yes we can.'

The chant starts somewhere in the back and takes a few moments to get traction. Then it fizzles out again.

The campaign officials decide it's time for a little pep-talk while the crowd waits for their candidate to speak in Chicago. A senior organiser comes to the microphone in front of the screens and speaks a few words in Spanish. Eventually he switches to English and recalls the night of the California primary in 1968. It was the night Bobby Kennedy was shot as he made his way through the kitchen of the Ambassador Hotel on his way to claim victory.

'Forty years ago was the last time California mattered in a presidential campaign and forty years ago people saw hope extinguished in Los Angeles when Bobby Kennedy was killed,' the official tells the crowd, 'That hope has been reignited again with Barack Obama.'

Before he can finish his speech, the crowd lets out a roar. Obama has just appeared on those giant screens. It is as if we are all in that crowded ballroom in Chicago. The candidate is waving to his supporters, and almost 3,000 kilometres away in Hollywood they wave back and chant: 'Yes we can'. The chanting makes it impossible to make out what Obama is saying on that podium. But eventually, a room that was once filled with the sound of Judy Garland, Joe Strummer and Richard Nixon is now full of the sound of Barack Obama in mid-sentence: ' … a campaign that has united Americans of all parties, from all backgrounds, from all races, from all religions, around a common purpose.'

With every pause and punchline there are increasingly ecstatic cheers from all races and religions here in the Avalon.

'We are the hope of the future, the answer to the cynics who tell us our house must stand divided, that we cannot come together, that we cannot remake this world as it should be.'

By and large, the people who walked into the Avalon that night were strangers to each other, swallowed up by a city of enclaves and ghettoes and its history of unresolved tension. But tonight, together, they will feel a moment of clarity and unity. Together, they get to press the reset button. Surrounded by each other, they can honestly believe the world just might begin again.

Yosi guides some of the camera crews down to the dance floor to watch the climax of the speech. The faces all around us are flushed with unchecked joy. A blonde woman close to the bar is hopping on both feet, looking a little too thin, a little too excited and perhaps a little too drunk. A group of black professionals in the centre of the crowd wearing sharp grey and black suits are punching the air as if they were cheering on a racehorse. Our camera finally settles on one slight young man with a thin goatee beard and red sweatshirt, who is waving an Obama sign with such abandon that he seems to be willing people to look at him, to validate his uncontrolled enthusiasm.

When the speech is over, the chanting begins again. Obama is shaking hands in Chicago and the crowd in the Avalon makes you feel that you are right there with him. Eventually, the screens go mute and the nightclub's sound system kicks in. The song they play is 'I Am Everyday People' by Arrested Development.

The young man with the goatee tells his story with such force that you can almost hear his teeth grind. He says his name is Taj and he has never worked on a campaign before: 'When he is our president, this world is going to change and that is why we are here tonight. This is something that has truly inspired me and I will take it with me for the rest of my life.'

Taj has taken his inspiration and passed it on to the rest of his family, including his 92-year-old great-aunt. Just the other day he sent her a letter telling her how excited he was to be working for Obama: 'She read that letter. She has voted in the last twenty elections as a Republican and she says she can't wait until November to go out and vote for Barack Obama.'

Taj's parents have come to the Avalon tonight. They are former radical activists basking in the reflected glory of their son's happiness. Together they are Moses and he is Joshua: 'I am here with my parents who were hippies in the '60s marching for civil rights and equal rights and everything and they have gotten involved in this campaign in the last two weeks because they have seen what it means to me and how inspirational it has been – not just Barack Obama, everyone who is working on his campaign because it is about us and that is different than anything we have seen in America ever.'

It is about us. We are the ones we have been waiting for. Yes we can.

These are the slogans that keep Obama's multi-racial Millennial army warm at night. Even as they seek to take over from the Moses generation, they steal their rhetoric of struggle and inclusion. To be fair to the Millennials, they have every right to embrace this language. They are, after all, the most diverse generation in American history.

When we use that word diverse, we are not talking about some progressive state of mind; we are referring to an astonishing fact of American life.

Two out of every five Americans born since 1982 is African-American, Latino, Asian or of mixed race. In other words, 40 per cent of Millennials are part of an ethnic minority, compared to just 25 per cent of the last two generations.

The word 'minority' is now increasingly inaccurate; large parts of the Sunbelt already have a Latino majority. By 2010, 77 per cent of children in New Mexico will have a distinctly ethnic identity, as will 53 per cent of kids in California. Between now and 2025, the number of states with an ethnic majority will increase from six to eighteen. By 2050, if current trends continue, white people will be the minority. More accurately, they will be just one of many minorities.

The changing face of America is partly explained by fertility patterns; in other words, who is having more kids. Since 2000, America's Latino and Asian populations have both increased by nearly a third and the African-American population has risen by 10 per cent. By contrast, there was just a one-per-cent increase in the number of white Americans. The ethnic transformation is also driven by historically high levels of immigration which look set to be maintained or increase; by the middle of the century, almost 20 per cent of Americans will be foreign-born.

There are some signs of inter-ethnic conflict, which we shall return to a little later, but there is also hard evidence of a multi-racial breakthrough in American life. The 2000 census found there were 3.1 million inter-racial couples in the United States, which is about six per cent of married couples.

What is more significant than the hard numbers is the trend: the number of inter-racial marriages increased by 65 per cent between 1990 and 2000. Racial boundaries are collapsing fastest on the Sunbelt, where most of those mixed marriages are taking place. California is home to one in ten of America's married couples but one in five of its inter-racial couples. More than one in 10 marriages are inter-racial in Arizona, New Mexico and Nevada.

The surge of inter-racial romance is helping to blur ethnic and racial boundaries. For the first time, the 2000 census allowed Americans to identify themselves as being of two or more races. That category that now includes 7.3 million Americans, or about three per cent of the population. It is expected that by the year 2050, 21 per cent of Americans will be multi-racial.

That trend is even greater among the Millennials; the 2000 census found that 41 per cent of the mixed-race population was under 18. Even the language young people use to categorise themselves is starting to evolve, partly in response to public figures like Tiger Woods, who describes himself as 'Cablinasian' (or a little bit Caucasian, African-American, Native American and Asian).

The Millennials are the driving force behind the blending of America. They are the most tolerant generation in American history, with 90 per cent reporting that they have a friend of a different race. Sixty per cent of 18- to 29-year-olds said that they had dated outside their racial group and 95 per cent said that they approved of relationships between black and whites. That may not sound like a huge breakthrough until you realise that as recently as 1987, less than half of all Americans took that view.

The tantalising possibility in all this is that decades of 'identity politics', in which insecurity and conflict forced Americans to cling to their tribe, is coming to an end. Perhaps age will trump race, as demographer Bill Frey suggests when he says: 'People under 40 are dating inter-racially. They are marrying inter-racially. Their identity with racial groups will not be nearly as strong as their tie to their generation.'

In truth, generation alone is not the only driving force behind America's inter-racial transition. Perhaps the biggest transformational pressure is the historic shift to the suburbs, and particularly the Sunbelt boomburbs. Frederick Jackson Turner said it was 'the crucible of the frontier' that Americanised the first waves of immigrants. Today, the Sunbelt Frontier is the crucible of a new American identity.

Remember how all the critics told us that suburban life lacked a civic gene because it was racially segregated? Well, the facts have changed. Not only are boomburbs the most dynamic parts of America, they are also becoming the most diverse. Forty-five of the 54 boomburbs have Latino populations that are bigger than the national average, and three-quarters have Asian populations that are above the average. One in 10 Americans are foreign-born, but in the boomburbs it is one in five.

There are boomburbs with little or no racial integration, but times are changing. There were just 41 African-Americans living in Gilbert back in 1980. Twenty years later, there were 2,000. The golden rule of life on the Sunbelt Frontier is that everything evolves and moderates. The boomburbs no longer represent a flight from the melting pot: they are the melting pot.

The growing diversity of suburban life is the next logical chapter in the classic American traditions of mobility and ambition. Americans still move in huge numbers – 40 million in 2005, according to US census estimates – and what is driving them is that same dream of a better piece of the America pie.

Just as the Irish in America moved out of their big urban ghettos in pursuit of 'lace-curtain-living' in the suburbs, African-Americans are doing the same. The black population of the suburbs increased by more than 26 per cent between 2000 and 2006.

Such is the lure of the new frontier that increasing numbers of new immigrants are following the pioneer trail and bypassing the cities altogether. About four in ten new immigrants are moving directly to the suburbs, according to the latest census figures, and the destinations of choice are predominantly in the South and the West. This is a striking break with the patterns of the past where immigrants usually bedded down in ethnic quarters of the big cities for at least a generation before moving out and up.

Might we have reached a tipping point? If you take the population boom in the Sunbelt, add in the growing power of ethnic groups and mix that up with the decline of the old coastal cities and Rustbelt states of the Midwest, you have a recipe for a political transformation.

The Great Dispersal of Americans has shifted more political power to the Sunbelt, giving them more votes in Congress and more influence in the presidential election process. Those states are increasingly young, diverse and moderate, and that is changing the political complexion of the Southwest. All this

137

means that the states of Nevada, Colorado, New Mexico and Arizona could be the gateway to a new era in American politics.

Even in the last presidential election, it was the Sunbelt as much as traditional battleground states of the Midwest which swung the 2004 election for George Bush. There were more than 120 million votes cast, but if Democrat John Kerry had picked up just 70,000 more votes in Nevada, New Mexico and Colorado, he would have been president.

Bush won New Mexico by less than one per cent, Nevada by less than three per cent and Colorado by less than five per cent. The same dynamic was at play four years before, when George Bush faced Al Gore. We all remember how tight it turned in Florida, but what people forget is that just 366 votes separated Gore and Bush in New Mexico in 2000.

In the 2008 election, the battlegrounds are what are known as the 'purple' states, where George Bush and John Kerry were separated by less than ten per cent of the vote in 2004. And the fiercest battles are for the purple states where the number of voters is increasing. The slowest-growing purple states are in the Midwest and tend to have large white majorities. The nine fastest-growing purple states are in the West and have a growing number of ethnic voters. The number of eligible voters in Nevada, for example, has increased by 27 per cent since 2000 and minorities make up half of that increase. Arizona has 20 per cent more voters and two-thirds of them are from minority groups.

As the ethnic vote becomes ever more important in American politics, the smiles on the faces of Democratic Party leaders get ever wider. In the 2006 mid-term election, Democrats won 69 per cent of the Hispanic vote. The trends are most pronounced among the recent group of immigrants, with surveys showing that foreign-born Latino voters are more than three times as likely to identify with the Democrats as with the Republicans. Polls also show that America's growing Asian population is starting to lean towards the Democrats. The impact is already being felt in Arizona, once a bulwark of fearsome Western conservatism. Now the state's Governor, Janet Napolitano, is a Democrat. She cruised to a 28-point victory in the 2006 mid-term elections, and her party picked up one of Arizona's four seats in the US Congress, erasing the Republicans' three-to-one advantage.

These trends offered real hope to the Democrats in the 2008 presidential cycle, and you would have assumed that Barack Obama would be the candidate most likely to capitalise on them. You certainly couldn't think of a better demonstration of the emerging inter-racial reality of Millennial America than the scene at the ballroom of the Avalon, and you could not imagine a better candidate to reflect it than Barack Obama. In a groundbreaking speech on race in March 2008, he examined his own remarkable inter-racial DNA and put it in the context of the American Joshua generation.

> I am the son of a black man from Kenya and a white woman from Kansas. I was raised with the help of a white grandfather who survived a Depression to serve in Patton's Army during World War II, and a white grandmother who worked on a bomber assembly line at Fort Leavenworth while he was overseas. I've gone to some of the best schools in America and lived in one of the world's poorest nations. I am married to a black American who carries within her the blood of slaves and slaveowners – an inheritance we pass on to our two precious daughters. I have brothers, sisters, nieces, nephews, uncles and cousins, of every race and every hue, scattered across three continents, and for as long as I live, I will never forget that in no other country on Earth is my story even possible.

139

You get the clear sense that Obama is most comfortable talking about a post-racial America. Coming into the 2008 election cycle, he was criticised by some prominent African-Americans for not speaking in the same charged language as black leaders of the Moses generation. He made no real effort to offer himself as a spokesperson for a coalition of black and brown Americans. But eventually he would we tripped up by the cracks in the shiny veneer of America's inter-racial transformation. Like any historic shift, this ethnic makeover is not without its tensions and contradictions. Obama's experience should be a warning to liberals, inside America and out, that history does not always move as fast as you would want it to.

—•—

The crowd in the Avalon nightclub were more interested in themselves than in the big screens on the stage but, in retrospect, they may have been distracted by collective self-regard. The sad truth for that rainbow of Obama supporters was that California slipped out of their grasp. As they doused themselves with alcohol, the screens were telling them that Hillary Clinton was going to win their state by a handy margin.

The sparkle had gone out of the Obama party by about 9.30 and it seemed like a good moment to go in search of some victorious Clinton supporters. Out of Hollywood, down the freeway, past downtown and the signs lead you to East Los Angeles, the Latino heartland. This is also Clinton country, a place where we would find a real whooping, humdinger of a victory party. At least you would have thought.

Inside Clinton's East L.A. headquarters, an elderly man is sweeping the floor. Two small groups of people are gathered around the TVs, one of which is tuned into the Spanish-language news programme. There is a trestle table in the corner still laden down with food, which is slowly congealing. One young volunteer approaches and explains that the small room was heaving with people just half an hour ago. 'People were tired,' she says. 'Now it is just the diehards.'

There is a small group in the corner of the room arranged around a petite elderly lady. She is smiling so hard that her eyes are partly submerged in a lifetime of creases. She radiates warmth across the room. When she begins to speak, her voice is hoarse and weak and she sounds weary.

'We know we have a long way to go between now and November,' she says. 'It's going to be a long haul.'

As she talks, a young man walks straight up to the old woman and grasps her hand. He turns back and says, 'You know who this is? This is Dolores Huerta. She is a legend in our community.' A woman pushes into the semi-circle of people surrounding the old woman and spreads out a copy of the biggest-selling Spanish language newspaper in Los Angeles. 'There she is.' She points to a full-page photograph of Dolores Huerta on stage with Hillary Clinton.

Delores tilts her head, and her smile twitches a little. She grasps her hands together in a gesture of modesty.

Dolores Huerta was brought to California from New Mexico by her mother in 1933. She grew up around the farms of the San Joaquin Valley where she saw the hard edge of anti-Hispanic prejudice. She co-founded the United Farm Workers Union with the legendary activist César Chávez in 1962. During a lifetime of protest, she was arrested 22 times and in 1988, her spleen was ruptured by a police baton during a demonstration in San Francisco. Such is her standing that any politician seriously seeking Latino votes courts Dolores Huerta. She has been making her mark on Democratic Party politics for more than four decades. She worked closely with Bobby Kennedy and was with him on the night that he was assassinated. She wears a necklace with the words 'Sí Se Puede' engraved on it. She and César Chávez had coined the phrase way back in 1972. It means

'Yes we can'. The cool kids may have been chanting it at the Avalon, but Dolores has lived it.

Dolores Huerta, a heroine of the Moses generation, had rejected the self-appointed leader of the Joshua generation, Barack Obama.

'Latinos know struggle and they feel Hillary has been with them. She has a long relationship with our community which Barack Obama doesn't have. People just don't know him. Hillary was out there in south Texas in her early twenties and she worked on all the big issues for our community, like educational reform and health care. Oh, and of course, jobs.'

Those issues, and the endorsement of legendary leaders like Dolores Huerta would send Latinos streaming to the polls in California to vote for Hillary Clinton. Even Latinos aged between 18 and 29 backed Clinton by huge margins (65 per cent), just as white Californians of the same age backed Obama by almost the same margin (63 per cent).

All this posed a real problem for Obama. After all, he is the first post-racial politician and California should be a state perfectly attuned to his message of generational change. It was a constant theme at his rallies in the days before Super Tuesday. At a giant gathering of UCLA students, the iconic figures of Caroline Kennedy and Oprah Winfrey were among thousands who turned out to anoint Obama. California's First Lady, Maria Shriver, was also there. She might be married to a Republican governor, but she is a member of the Kennedy clan, a Democrat at heart. She declared, 'If Barack Obama were a state, he'd be California.' Writing about the event, a *New York Times* journalist declared that Obama's campaign 'seemed to have a monopoly on what is hip, young and glamorous in California'.

He may have had. But hip and glamorous didn't cut it in California, or in every other state with a big Latino population. Obama lost primaries and caucuses in the key Sunbelt states of Nevada, Texas, New Mexico, Arizona and California, and in each of these contests, Latino voters plumped for Hillary Clinton by margins of between 60 and 70 per cent. Even the young opted to stick with their own community, rather than follow a broader youthful surge towards Obama.

The margins suggest that the apparently seemless shift into a post-racial future will be more complicated than it first appeared. An often unacknowledged source of racial tension is the territorial or economic rivalry between African-Americans and Latinos, particularly in huge cities such as Los Angeles. That may well have played a part in Obama's poor showing in the Sunbelt, even if it is not a popular thing for politicians or their advisers to say.

Hillary Clinton's Hispanic pollster, Sergio Bendixen, sparked controversy when he said that 'the Hispanic voter ... has not shown a lot of willingness or affinity to support black candidates.' It may have been a crude generalisation, but some credible observers believe there a nugget of truth in it. It is not necessarily racism at work; it has more to do with the rivalry of two groups in American society who have struggled harder than most for their share of the American dream.

Though ethnic tension played a part in Obama's poor showing among Latinos, economics was the key factor. Consider Dolores Huerta, for example. There was no racism in her decision to back Hillary Clinton. Clinton's long-standing ties to the Latino community might have influenced her, but her instinctual aversion to Obama was a factor of her bitter experience of struggle; she has known too much heartbreak and failure to buy into his soaring rhetoric. At a time when America heads towards recession and hard-pressed Latino families face an uncertain future, leaders like Dolores Huerta will back experience over hope.

In many ways, what mattered for Latinos in the 2008 election was class rather than race or generation. They had much in common with working-class whites who shared their economic insecurities, and that showed up in their voting preferences in states like California. Away from the rich, hip and glamorous California we all know so well, Obama faltered. He won a big majority among Californians who earn more than $100,000, but Hillary Clinton had overwhelming backing from those who earned less than $50,000.

Take the highway inland from Los Angeles and you come to another California. San Bernardino and Riverside are where many of those suburban immigrants had fled to. Their house prices are lower, but so, too, are their incomes. In a property-based recession, 'the inland areas are full of people struggling to hold onto middle-class status' says Dowell Myers, a demographer at the University of Southern California; 'they are not risk-takers'. In Riverside County, 59 per cent of voters backed Hillary Clinton, which was almost exactly the same proportion as in San Bernardino.

The young people we met in the Avalon represent an exciting new force for progress in the United States which, in the long term, is almost certainly a transformational change. But, for the moment, dreams are often sacrificed at the altar of necessity. The Latino families of San Bernardino, Riverside and East Los Angeles show us that the course of this American reinvention is being shaped by doubt as much as by hope.

Does that mean that Latinos, the fastest-growing ethnic group in America, will opt for conservative politicians above liberal reformers like Barack Obama? It is a possibility worth considering for a moment. After all, George Bush won two elections with a great deal of help from Latinos; 44 per cent of them backed him in 2004. Some have suggested that they played a bigger factor in his re-election than evangelical voters. Bush's political guru, Karl Rove, had a longstanding dream of giving Republicans a permanent majority among Latinos by appealing to their conservatism on social issues, their religious devotion and their patriotism.

While it is worth considering the possibility that Latinos might move back toward the Republicans in these tough economic times, it is not worth considering for too long. As they have played to anti-immigrant sentiment in recent years, Republicans have driven Latinos deeper into the Democrat camp. Even John McCain, who is relatively liberal on immigration, has publicly said that 'the Hispanic vote is turning against us in very large numbers.'

The tide has almost certainly turned decisively in the ethnic politics of America. Democrats can increasingly depend on the support of the fastest-growing sections of the electorate, particularly in the swing states of the Southwest. There is every reason to believe that the boundaries between the races are slowly disintegrating in the face of an advancing generation for whom race no longer shapes the boundaries of their lives.

The 2008 election sends mixed messages about the speed of this ethnic transformation. In the first place, the range of candidates reminds us of just how diverse America has become; among the runners in this race for the White House have been a black man, a woman, a Mormon, an Italian-American and an Hispanic. In spring 2008, John McCain let it be known that among his list of potential running mates was the 36-year-old Indian-American Governor of Louisiana, Piyush 'Bobby' Jindal. Yet, faced with possibility of their first inter-racial president, a significant number of Americans have recoiled. In the face of reinvention, they have chosen to retreat.

Sheer force of numbers means that America will be reinvented, whether the next president is a white man or a black man – but the issue is momentum. How fast can America extricate itself from the historic tensions that have fed the flames of 'identity politics'? We should hold on to the images of that intoxicating crowd at the Avalon, but we would do well to listen to the hard-headed realism of Dolores Huerta.

Hard economic times are creating fear among those who live on the margins of American society. Just as the rise of a multiracial reality is helping the reinvention of America, the growing insecurity of America's hardest-pressed citizens is its biggest obstacle. Reinvention requires people to think beyond their own tribal identity, to feel solidarity with people simply on the basis of human empathy and not ideology or race. Let's see what happens when the bright lights of reinvention collide with the dark shadow of recession.

Part Three:
The Problems

7.
Fullerton – The Economics of Fear

The fire in the hearth is roaring and crackling and pouring forth warmth and welcome. John Coffman collected the wood himself, just yesterday. His speech carries a trace of his native Arkansas, and his thick, snow-white beard and weathered baseball cap speak to you of foraging and fixing amid mountains and country streams. But John lives in a different sort of wilderness – a rambling forest of low-slung ranch houses hemmed in by the torrential flow of the Orange and Santa Ana Freeways.

By contrast, John's wife Grayce appears to be in her natural California habitat. She is a child of the post-war boom, which sent millions of city folks into the suburbs of Orange County. She has no pretence, no sharp edges. There is a simple, almost dreamy elegance about Grayce, and she has kind eyes, full of hope for a temperate autumn among neighbours and family.

Grayce and John moved into this house in the suburb of Fullerton 31 years ago. It was built in an age when families still gathered around a dining table out of sight of the television. There is an air of formality in the front room, which is a museum to three decades of family life, full of knick-knacks, souvenirs, holiday snaps and heirlooms. But the farther you get from the front door, the more casual and unadorned the house becomes. Out back, the pool catches the decaying glow of the evening sun which casts lengthening shadows over the heavy plastic sheet that covers the pool furniture. Aside from the buzz of the light planes on their final approach to the nearby airport, there is calm here, comfort.

Grayce's hands offer up the first sign of trouble. Ribbons of skin have come away from her palms, parting company with the angry, livid flesh beneath. She is suffering from eczema, which her doctor says has been triggered by stress. It is the same stress that forced John onto anti-depressants, on top of the medicine he takes to regulate his heart. John is mightily fed up with the fatigue and occasional hallucinations all this medication has brought on.

The Coffmans live with their six grandchildren, two sausage-shaped dachshunds and a seven-year-old goldfish called Jaws. The oldest grandchild, Brittany, is twenty-two and studies art history at a nearby college. The only boy, Jay, is an eleven-year-old sports fan with Attention Deficit Disorder. In between are Lindsay, Sarah, Katie and Megan. The children should be with their mother, John and Grayce's daughter, but she and her husband developed a serious drug problem. One day, things got so bad that John called the cops and took custody of his grandchildren.

Grayce and John tell the story with the minimum of detail, suggesting unresolved pain, but they seem entirely comfortable with the enormous responsibility they are shouldering in what should be their retirement years. They raised four kids of their own, and now offer warmth and sanctuary to the next generation.

'I don't hunt and I don't fish. We do this. We take care of kids,' says John. Before he can get out another word, Grayce says, 'We have never had an empty nest.'

Raising six kids did not cause the eczema or the depression. What's haunting John and Grayce Coffman is the nightmare of foreclosure. Since the letter arrived from the mortgage company two months ago, they have lived every waking moment with the prospect of losing their home.

The maths are brutally simple. They are unemployed and receive social welfare payments of $5,200 per month to care for their grandchildren. Their mortgage payments now stand at $4,500 per month. The couple have about $1,400 saved for a rainy day. They never thought it would it would rain quite as hard as this.

'If they want to take my house, they will have to take me, the goldfish, the dogs and the kids,' says Grayce

It is a rare and rehearsed statement of defiance. As she and John talk through their problems by the side of their pool, she spends most of her time staring down at the tiles on the patio with that dreamy, faraway look in her eyes again. But the dream has soured and there is no waking refuge from it.

'It is just surreal, just a bad dream,' she says, adding in a quieter tone: 'How did we get in this mess?'

The answer to that question is a combination of misfortune and recklessness, although back in the days of a booming property market their behaviour would not have seemed all that reckless. Millions of Americans did what the Coffmans did; they took out huge loans against the rising value of their house, and spent it as if the boom would be a permanent feature of their lives.

At least the Coffmans used the money for legitimate purposes, taking out loans to expand their house and make room for their six grandchildren. Then in 2005, John's radiator repair business got into trouble and the Coffmans borrowed a little over $550,000 from America's biggest home lender, Country-wide Financial. The radiator shop continued to falter and when John got sick, Grayce wound up the business. The couple were left with no assets and a mountain of debt. Despite making a total of $50,000 in payments, their debt to Countrywide grew to $590,000 within two years. In a desperate bid to keep up with their payments, they borrowed more money and sank deeper into a hole of their own making.

Grayce knows how badly they screwed up, but she still feels that her family has been trapped by the devil in the detail of the loans they took out. She says there was no reasonable way that she or her husband could have known how quickly their debts would rise, as unpaid interest was added on to the rapidly increasing principal.

'It started out at 550,000, then it became 558,000 and then it was 560,000. We couldn't understand it. We take some of the blame for this, but the people making the loans should have taken the blame as well.'

'We have been to bankruptcy lawyers and property lawyers,' John says, 'and they all say we don't understand this loan, so how would we?'

The Coffmans' last hope comes in the form of Connie Der Torossian, who works for the Fair Housing Council of Orange County. She is a former mortgage adviser who now mediates between homeowners facing repossession and the companies from which they borrowed. Her office has been overwhelmed by a surge of enquiries from families in big trouble, but the Coffmans seem to have found a special place in her heart.

The Coffmans greet her like a favourite daughter when she arrives at their house and she responds in kind. But anger rises to her face as she begins to talk. Connie says the big lenders are working flat out to cope with the nightmare they helped to create, but she can't believe they didn't see the warnings. The loans they offered were often designed to confuse borrowers. In many cases, loans were made to people with no earthly way of carrying the long-term burden. And yet no one shouted stop.

'This is an expensive place to buy, and sub-prime mortgages opened up the market to first-time buyers who couldn't really afford houses selling in the 600,000s. It just couldn't go on.'

When Connie is asked why no one spoke up, she laughs, quickly and bitterly, before speaking at a higher pitch.

'I did. I could see this was going to happen.'

So why didn't they listen?

'Because things were good,' she says, regaining her calm. 'People were making a lot of money.'

Then she pauses, as if she is about to cross some invisible barrier.

'Greed played a part in all this.'

Connie's home turf is ground zero for the sub-prime crisis that has shaken America. Almost half of the 20 biggest sub-prime lenders in the United States were based in Orange County. They targeted aspiring homeowners who were considered to be too great a risk to get loans from mainstream banks, and for a while their business was unbelievably good, especially in their own backyard. One in five houses bought in Orange County in 2006 was bought with sub-prime mortgage funds and some began referring to the suburbs south of Los Angeles as 'mortgage alley'.

There was a nasty, brutish edge to the sub-prime boom in the working-class neighbourhoods of Orange County where lenders targeted Latino neighbourhoods they knew had been shunned by the mainstream financial institutions. The highest concentration of sub-prime loans in the county were in the poor, ethnic districts of Santa Ana where 75 per cent of the home loans were sub-prime. The easy money had a name in these neighbourhoods: *la droga*. The narcotic thrill of owning a house with no money down masked the ugly realities of 'piggyback loans', low teaser payments, adjustable-rate loans and prepayment penalties. You got the money, but you would never understand the terms, particularly if English was your second language.

The sub-prime contagion spread across the Sunbelt, turning the property game into a new gold rush. At one point, it was estimated that one in every fifty-three adults in California had a real estate licence. In Las Vegas, such was the demand for the services of mortgage-brokers that 'every stripper, waiter and bartender on the Strip had a broker's license', one such part-time broker told *Newsweek* magazine.

One of the driving forces behind the property boom was speculation. A house was not something to be lived in, it was something to be bought and sold as quickly, to be 'flipped'. At the height of the madness, there was a TV show called *Flip that House*, and a web site called condoflip.com with the motto 'Bubbles are for Bathtubs'.

The property gold rush helped to sustain the American economy in the testing times that followed 9/11. Between 2001 and 2005, 40 per cent of all jobs created in the US were related to housing. At its height, the property boom was creating 30,000 jobs every month.

As homeowners watched house prices head towards the stratosphere, they began to do what the Coffmans had done and borrowed against the rising value of their homes; the house would play the role of ATM, providing a ready source of cash that was as safe as … well, houses. Again, the temptation was strongest in Sunbelt states like California where 30 per cent of cars sold in 2006 were financed with 'home equity' loans.

Americans had become the most prolific borrowers on Earth and no one in power seemed the slightest bit concerned. The financial gurus in New York and Washington were too busy crowing about the unprecedented stability of the American economy. Ben Bernanke, the man who would go on to lead the US Federal Reserve, had a name for it: 'the Great Moderation'. Somebody forget to tell the homeowners and car-buyers and part-time mortgage brokers of the Sunbelt about the moderation part of the equation.

The web of sub-prime insanity began to unravel in early 2007 as repayments began to bite and house prices started to fall. The number of people losing their homes through foreclosure in Orange County rose to its highest level in at least twenty years in the first quarter of 2008. A consumer watchdog called the Center for Responsible Lending estimated that almost one in four sub-prime mortgages made in Orange County in 2007 would end in foreclosure, which would represent seven per cent of all the homes bought in the county that year.

Right across the Sunbelt, the price of houses nosedived, particularly in the once-booming market of Phoenix, which had been a magnet for investors trying to flip properties for a quick buck. By the spring of 2008, one estate agent in the Phoenix suburb of Goodyear was so desperate for business that she was offering a limo tour of investment properties and a free brunch to follow. In Las Vegas, a group of eternally optimistic property dealers created a sightseeing tour called the 'Vegas Foreclosure Express' which gave potential investors a chance to view repossessed houses which had been put back on the market.

The great property rush may have ended in farce but it brought incalculable pain. For citizens' advocates like Connie Der Torossian, it inspires deep, abiding anger. But if Connie has big questions to pose, Grayce and John Coffman don't. They understand that millions of other Americans like them were seduced into high-risk borrowing. They know that an ever-expanding pool of homeowners face foreclosure, just like them. But they are not as mad as hell. When asked why such as thing could happen, in this day and age, John seems confused.

'Really,' he says, shaking his head, 'that is a good question: How is it happening to so many people?'

John might just as well be talking about a flood or a storm, some natural disaster. There is not a trace of anger in his voice when he asks that question. Grayce is equally lacking in resentment. Her eyes betray the crushing burden of her ordeal as they drift towards the middle distance; they even teared up briefly when Connie arrived at the door. But she refuses to be riled, since she has cannot afford anything but the most uncomplicated emotions. Ask her why she refuses to give in to resentment and she says: 'Anger is not going to get us anywhere. Anyway, when your silences are filled with worry, there is no room for faith.'

John and Grayce seem puzzled by questions about their political views. They come across as conservative but non-judgemental and Republican in the vaguest sense. They are disconnected rather than apathetic. They draw no moral or political lesson from their slide into despair; they seek no help from politicians. When John is asked if his troubles have made him more interested in the coming presidential election, he offers a strangely emphatic 'no', as if can't bear the thought of false hope. Grayce is only slightly more optimistic.

'Politicians are politicians,' she says, lowering her eyes and throwing a little ironic glance towards her husband, 'but if they do what they promise, we will get back on track.'

'This is going to be a wait-and-see situation,' John says with finality. 'We just really don't know.'

Of all the sad things about the Coffmans' ordeal, the saddest is their profound sense of isolation. Despite Connie Der Torossian's intervention, they seem to really believe they are alone and so have ordered their emotions around that fact. Anger would be a wasted energy. Just as it would be pointless to rage against a departing storm that tore off your roof, it makes no sense to the Coffmans to ask bitter questions about an economic system that could sanction predatory lending and encourage reckless borrowing. The Coffmans are at one with their suffering because they believe they will eventually prevail. If not, they will just get on with it. There is no one to blame.

The Coffmans may be naïve in their faith, but they did not deserve the tidal wave of viciousness that came their way. The *Orange County Register* published their story just before Christmas 2007, setting off a nasty wave of commentary across the United States. Within hours of the *Register* article being published, one of America's leading conservative bloggers, Michelle Malkin, had posted her response, in which she said acidly that if this 'story doesn't send your blood pressure through the roof and have you shouting "Boo Freaking Hoo!" at the top of your lungs, I don't know what will.' Within weeks, the Coffmans were featured on a nationally syndicated list of the 'Top 5 Most Ridiculous Mortgage Borrower Stories of 2007'.

The *Orange County Register* website received almost a hundred responses to the original article and almost every one was negative. What these critics chose to see was a big family on social welfare who had made reckless choices and now wanted sympathy. Their story was 'bogus heart-tugging drivel', said one commentator. 'Geez, the entire story just makes me sick!' said another. Clearly having gorged on the milk of human kindness, one contributor asked how anyone could 'feel sorry for these incredibly shallow, shortsighted, immature, non-thinking knuckleheads.'

As the commentary focussed on John and Grayce's decision to take custody of their grandchildren, the tone got darker. One contributor wrote a 'six-point to do' list for the Coffmans which included advice to 'get off the government dole; we're tired of paying for your kids, loser!!!' 'I have no sympathy for these folks. NONE,' read another posting. 'I have no doubt they failed to teach their own children responsibility, which is why they have so many adopted grandchildren.'

With varying degrees of outrage, the contributors advised the Coffmans to get a job and give up their house (or be forced out) to pay for the debt. A constant theme was a fierce resistance to any state aid for the family. 'I'll be damned if a penny of my tax goes to help these kinds of family out!', said one contributor, while another warned that 'if they get bailed out by some bleeding hearts, that will just really get under my skin.'

Once again, we are reminded of what it is like to live in a frontier society which worships self-reliance. Good things happen to good people. Failure is a reminder that you are not trying hard enough. This is easy to believe in the good times, but when times get tough, failure is harder to rationalise. When someone just as decent and hard-working as you gets into difficulty, obvious questions arise. Did they fail or did the system fail them? Can people like me really have faith in the American dream?

It is easier to cope with doubt if you can blame bad times on the personal shortcomings of weak people. The more you believe in their failure, the more secure you become about your own security and personal virtue. Take the Coffmans as an example: by focussing on their recklessness, the critics turned this family tragedy into a morality tale. It served to reassure us that bad things like foreclosure happen only to bad people.

With their bitter words, the critics dispelled any lingering doubts about the American dream. 'This country offers Life, Liberty and the Pursuit of Happiness,' wrote one of the Coffmans' critics, 'not three hots and a cot. Maybe the children WILL learn from this experience IF the family is displaced. We work for what we have and respect the property of others.'

By heaping condemnation on the Coffmans, the critics removed the need to answer the other troubling questions posed by this family's misfortune: what kind of company would extend such dangerous loans? What kind of financial system would encourage such lending? By attacking the Coffmans, the critics vented pent-up rage at the unfolding sub-prime insanity in a way that would not cast doubt over the unregulated economic freedom that spawned it.

What was significant about the backlash was the absence of solidarity from those who faced similar choices and challenges to the Coffmans. Many of the contributors identified themselves as struggling middle-class homeowners. Perhaps the most unsettling comment came from a woman who described herself as a 'a single mommy'. She said she would love the resources the Coffmans had access to: 'This story makes me madder every time I read it. I am glad they are not my neighbors because I really don't think I would be able to keep my mouth shut.'

This is the dark side of America's egalitarian impulse. People desperately need to feel that they are competing on a level playing field, so there is an enormous opposition to any group which demands an extra advantage, for whatever reason. That fierce resistance comes in many forms, including objections to preferences for racial minorities, and it seems to intensify in times of recession. The harder you have to struggle, the more you resent handouts to others.

It is not that Americans are less generous than other nationalities. Seventy per cent of American households make charitable contributions every year, donating an average of three and a half per cent of their income. Total charitable giving in the United States now stands at $260 billion a year, which is double what it was in 1995. But while Americans are more philanthropic than ever, they pay less tax and their government spends less on social programmes than most other developed nations. Individuals still want to have a say in who is deserving, rather than leaving it to the collective to make the decision.

In the Coffmans' case, the verdict was swift and brutal. The family were easy targets for resentment and rage, but they were also the wrong targets. They made mistakes, but they are a decent, generous and honourable family. There was no calculation in their decision to go public with their story. They asked for nothing, not charity and not a government handout. They were not complainers, just the opposite; in their eyes, endurance was the ultimate virtue.

Just occasionally, a ray of light shone on the dark portrait painted by the critics. A former neighbour of the Coffmans wrote to the *Orange County Register* and described them as 'the most giving people in the universe! They have never asked for charity or any type of financial bailout from anyone and have always tried to simply make ends meet! Even they will admit that they have made some financial mistakes along the way, but to suggest that they did so out of greed is simply ridiculous.' This tribute to the Coffmans was the exception: scorn was the rule.

What happened to this family points to a historic volatility in

American public life. The people of the United States 'are liable to swift and vehement outbursts of feeling,' wrote the great Belfast-born historian James Bryce in the late 19th century. 'Americans have what chemists call low specific heat; they grow warm suddenly and cool as suddenly.'

Bad times tend to lead to outbursts of moral panic. Tremendous energy is spent searching for villains and heroes, which tends to weaken the common ground between normal, flawed mortals. Americans are encouraged to cling to the certainties of their lives, like nationalism or race. Tribal loyalties become more important. Society divides into sub-sets. Sympathy is rationed.

You can see that tendency in the way people reacted to the Coffmans, but can we draw a broader conclusion here? Does the bitter, anti-social impulse we have just seen at work in Orange County threaten to overwhelm the renewal of America's civic instincts we have witnessed all across the Sunbelt Frontier? Because if it did, all our talk of reinvention and realignment would be premature. We need to work out just how bad the bad times really are, and just how much they will change the perpetual certainties of American life.

—•—

America has only two social classes: the middle class and the rich. There is no upper class, lower middle class, nouveau riche, bourgeoisie or peasantry. Most emphatically, there is no working class. If you strive, you are middle-class, whether you live in a trailer park in Kentucky or a big suburban house in Arizona.

But the definition of rich has become a lot more elastic in recent years. Not too long ago, if you could afford luxury without feeling pain, then you were rich. But luxury became a mass market, and you needed a lot more money to feel special. In 2005 alone, 227,000 Americans became millionaires. There are now as many millionaires in North Carolina (population 8.8 million) as there are in India (population 1,130 million). Not even a billion dollars buys you exclusivity any more. Back in 1985, there were just 13 billionaires in the United States. Now there are more than a thousand.

Spare a sympathetic thought for the genuinely rich American. Their luxury yacht is no longer the biggest in the marina and their private jet has to jostle for a parking space. What they really need is a smaller and more exclusive club to become members of. According to Robert Frank of the *Wall Street Journal,* that club has become its own country. In his best-seller, *Richistan,* he says that the wealthiest Americans were 'building a self-contained world, with its own health-care system (concierge doctors), travel system (private jets, destination clubs) and language. ("Who's your household manager?") They had created their own breakaway republic — one I called Richistan.'

During his travels in Richistan, Frank came across companies selling $600,000 watches and $320,000 cars and $47 million private jets. He meets the property billionaire who has two almost identical Rolls Royces in his driveway. 'The two-ton one, that's my restaurant car,' the billionaire tells Frank. 'You get a better parking space [from the valets].' All told, Franks says, America's richest .5 per cent spend $650 billion a year, which is about equal to total household spending in Italy.

So, Richistan is doing pretty well. But what about those left behind in that middle-class nation called America? According to the US census, prosperity touched the lives of almost all Americans between 1993 and 2003. During that decade, the bottom fifth of US society saw their average income rise by 13 per cent, but, apart from a slight drop in poverty in 2006, the good news ended there.

By almost every measure, the gap between rich and poor in the United States has widened by a historic degree in recent decades. If you were in the top fifth of earners in 1973, you earned 10 times as much as someone in the bottom fifth. By 2003, you would be earning almost 15 times as much.

But it is among the super-rich that things begin to get crazy. The richest one per cent of Americans now earns roughly twenty per cent of all income and controls thirty-three per cent of all the wealth. In fact, they have more money and assets than the bottom 90 per cent of Americans put together. The last time there was such a concentration of wealth in the hands of America's super-rich was at the tail end of the 'Gilded Age', just after World War I.

The citizens of Richistan have done very well out of the drive towards privatisation, deregulation and free markets which characterised the so-called Great Moderation. Chief executives and hedge fund managers became the new Rockefellers and Vanderbilts, and they kept much more of their income thanks to the tax breaks of the Bush years. The breathtaking inequality of all this was exposed by Warren Buffet, the world's third-richest man, during a speech in June 2007. He revealed he had paid 18 per cent tax on his income the previous year. His secretary paid 30 per cent. He earned $46 million; his secretary had an income of $60,000. Could this be the same America which President Lincoln promised in the Gettysburg Address would be 'dedicated to the proposition that all men are created equal'?

In any other Western nation, such a yawning chasm between rich and poor would have led to reform, if not rebellion. There have been some stirrings of a populist revolt in Washington in the recent past. One of the most effective American political speeches of recent years came from Virginia Senator Jim Webb in January 2007. In the Democratic response to President Bush's State of the Union address, he said that the average corporate chief executive made 20 times what the average worker did when he graduated from college – but now it's nearly 400 times more. 'In other words,' Webb said, 'it takes the average worker more than a year to make the money that his or her boss makes in one day.'

North Carolina Senator John Edwards staked his presidential ambitions in 2008 on the notion that there were 'two Americas'. He cast the election as 'a choice between corporate power and the power of democracy'. He told middle-class America that it was being being ravaged by corporate abuse: 'The truth is that corporate greed is stealing your children's future as sure as I'm standing here.' The fact that a mainstream Democratic candidate like Edwards would adopt such challenging rhetoric is a sign of the growing appetite for change in America. But Edwards departed early from the 2008 presidential race, proving that there are big obstacles to any populist uprising.

The first limitation is the American definition of inequality. What is traditionally meant by 'equality' in the US is equality of opportunity. In other words, every citizen is entitled to an equal shot at the American dream, but not necessarily an equal share of America's wealth. Rich people are an inspiration in the United States in a way they will never be in Europe. They are reminders that all the striving and pursuing has a tangible pay-off. In the words of tycoon Ted Turner, 'life is a game and money is how we keep score'. By that definition, the visible gap between rich and poor becomes a running total that can be changed during the course of the game as long as you think like a champion.

Less than one in three Americans think that the state should reduce income disparities, and that is because they tend to see inequality as a matter of individual performance rather than a systems failure. Recent opinion polls suggest that this sentiment is hardening even as inequality has grown. Pew researchers found that the number blaming outside factors for failure fell from 41 per cent in 1988 to 32 per cent in 2002.

But before we pronounce the populist cause dead, it is worth looking at the fine print of the American definition of equality. Remember, Americans do not believe in equality of outcome, but they do believe passionately in equality of opportunity: everyone must get an equal shot. The gap

163

between rich and poor is acceptable only if the poor have a chance of catching up.

This is what we mean when we talk of an American dream: the notion that the United States is a land of opportunity where each successive generation will do better than the last. The dream is, in the words of Texas political scientist Cal Jillson, the 'gyroscope of American life'. If, for some reason, this guarantee of upward mobility was removed from life, America would be diminished. And what would happen then? Would the players demand a change in the way the game was played?

There are signs that the American dream has reached a roadblock. The statistics reveal that social mobility has begun to suffer as the gap between rich and poor has widened. Millions of poor Americans still climb out of the ranks of poverty each year, but not enough to validate the grand aspirations of the dream. In 2008, the Pew Research Centre released a ground-breaking report on economic mobility and found that the United States is now less economically mobile than many other rich countries. The capacity of the poorest children to do better than their parents is now considerably weaker in America than it is in Denmark, Norway, Finland, Sweden or the United Kingdom. In America, there is a 42 per cent chance that if a father is stuck in the bottom fifth of earners, his son will get stuck there too. In Denmark, the equivalent odds are 25 per cent; in the UK, it's 30 per cent.

No matter how you define equality, no matter how you view success or failure, there is undeniably a weakness at the heart of the American dream, and more and more Americans realise it. At the beginning of our journey, we noted the conflict between public gloom and private optimism in the most recent snapshot of US public opinion. But don't let the private happiness distract us from the headline: public gloom in the United States is sowing the seeds of change.

In April 2008, a CBS/*New York Times* opinion poll found that more Americans believed their country was off track than at any time since the question had first been asked in 1991. Buried in the detail of the survey were answers that cast doubt over the prevalence of American dream. Just 46 per cent of parents said that they expected their children to enjoy a better standard of living than they had, a ten per cent drop since 2005. When asked in general terms about prospects for the next generation, just one in three of all those surveyed said that they would live better than people do today.

This growing sense of pessimism is a response to a sizeable economic shock and years of growing inequality, and it looks like it could be the beginning of a shift in American priorities. Whatever the Coffman case told us, the opinion polls suggest that Americans are beginning to reconsider their relationship with failure and inequality.

We know that the critics in Orange County firmly opposed government handouts for homeowners burdened with debt. But in that CBS News/*New York Times* poll in 2008, 53 per cent said that the government should help those coping with rising interest rates. There were also signs in the same survey that attitudes to government were shifting. Fifty-eight per cent of those surveyed said that households making more than $250,000 should pay more tax, while 43 per cent of those surveyed said that they would prefer a larger government that provided more services (the number supporting that idea has never been higher).

As you might expect, the trends are most pronounced among the Millennials, who have become increasingly worried about economic decline (the economy ranked well above Iraq as the number one issue for young people in the early stages of the 2008 presidential election). While three out of four young Americans say that they still believe in the American dream, this generation is keenly aware of its limitations. In a poll published in the summer of 2007, just one in four 17- to 29-year-olds said that their generation would be better off than their parents'.

If there is fear of an uncertain future among Millennials, there is no bitterness. You do not hear angry populist rhetoric from this generation. Instead, what you detect is a spirit of adaptation. Where previous generations lusted after well-paid, secure jobs that would last a lifetime, the Millennials' career path is, in the words of one commentator, 'more like a maze than a straight line'. Young Americans expect frequent job changes and a 'limited liability' relationship with their employers. Where Baby Boomers felt betrayed by the disappearance of lifetime guarantees, Millennials accept that as a starting point.

What young Americans are becoming increasingly intolerant of are poverty and inequality. In contrast to previous generations, they know more about and care more about these problems. In a 2004 poll, 84 per cent of Millennials said that the gap between rich and poor had grown over the previous two decades, and 94 per cent thought that was a bad thing.

Just as 9/11 was a defining event in the lives of Millennials, so was Hurricane Katrina, which brutally exposed the fault lines of race and poverty. It was a media spectacle without parallel and the fifth most closely followed story of the last twenty years in the United States. It was an event which, according to an editorial in the *Los Angeles Times*, might well prove to be 'a watershed in the debate over poverty, largely because it provided a window into the life of the poor that was more visceral and intimate than most Americans ever witness'.

The abject failure of state agencies in New Orleans may have further degraded faith in government among some Americans, but not among the Millennials. It seems only to have increased their appetite for an official response to poverty and inequality. A year after Katrina, a survey found that 'transitional Millennials' (those between the ages of 18 and 22) were more likely than any other age group to favour governmental action to reduce economic differences among Americans.

With each successive poll of young Americans, there is fresh evidence that we are arriving at a turning point. Millennials are just as self-reliant and individualistic as previous generations, if not more so, but they want collective solutions to problems long ignored by their leaders. That's great news for liberal groups like the Center for American Progress, which published a remarkable poll in May 2008. Among many other questions, it asked if the government should spend more on health care and education and other social services, even if that meant raising taxes. The Millennials said yes by margins not seen in the 20 years these questions have featured in opinion polls. The study also found that the number of young people who wanted the government to provide more services had jumped by 25 per cent in the space of a decade.

The surveys confirm what we already knew about the Millennials: they want civic solutions to America's problems. They may worry about the long-term health of their nation but have none of the caustic fear which has eaten away at America during past crises. In their particular balance of Frontier and Ritual, self-reliance and solidarity pose no contradictions.

The Millennial instincts will eventually collide with the fearful streak in the American psyche. You could argue they already have in the 2008 election. As he battled Hillary Clinton in Rustbelt states like Ohio and Pennsylvania, Barack Obama made a cack-handed attempt to describe the frustration of declining working-class communities. He used the word 'bitter' to describe them, and, in the process, he deepened their feeling of isolation and inflamed their sense of grievance. It was a reminder that reinvention in America can be a messy, angry business.

To understand the speed and momentum of the unfolding transformation, we have to set the potential of the Millennials against dark, competing instincts that linger in America's subconscious. It is hard for outsiders to make sense of the raging fear that often seems to contaminate American life, particularly when it is directed at people like the Coffmans. But there are reasons why people hide behind anger or ideology, race or tribe. There are reasons why even rational Americans would jealously guard the spirit of the frontier.

8.
Tombstone – Stirring the Melting Pot

Carmen Mercer is itching to go. Lunch service is over at the O.K. Café and she wants to get the hell out of Tombstone. By day, she serves up half-pound buffalo burgers, and by night she defends freedom on the boundary with Mexico.

Carmen pulls her silver Chevy pick-up out of its parking space and winds her way through the streets of this legendary Arizona town. 'The town too tough to die' has been consumed by make-believe. Just a few blocks along Allen Street, between the O.K. Corral and Big Nose Kate's saloon, the actors recreate gunfights from frontier days for the benefit of the tourists. Carmen drives away from the staged drama with a real-life Colt .45 holstered in her custom leather gun belt.

Carmen Mercer is vice-president of a self-appointed border militia, the Minutemen, and also their chief fundraiser and national recruiter. She is a big noise in the movement against illegal immigration, but seems to relish the chance to be just another volunteer patrolling that border. After all, that is what the Minutemen are all about: putting patriotic bodies on that frontier to raise an alarm and to call attention to the invasion of America. Ultimately, Carmen feels that the federal government will be forced to build a tall wall along the entire 2,000-mile border from the Pacific Ocean to the Gulf of Mexico. But for now, she knows her place, and it is in that silver Chevy driving towards Mexico.

'It's not the immigration we are against; it is the illegal side of it.'

Carmen is dressed in a black Minutemen T-shirt and blue jeans. She is small and has a boyish blonde haircut. She is in her early fifties but has the air of a studious teenager.

'How can you come into a country, sneak into a country, and then expect that you can have that American dream?'

There is something about the clipped, efficient way Carmen pronounces the letter 's' which gives her away. She is not from around these parts. She was born and raised in a small town near Cologne in Germany. She came to Ohio as a 17-year-old student in the 1970s, and after meeting the US soldier who would become her husband, she moved from base to base, from Florida to North Carolina to New Mexico and then to Arizona.

Eventually Carmen divorced and moved to Tombstone in 1992, taking over the O.K. Café a couple of years later. She had no hard and fast plans to become a US citizen until she got involved in local town politics. She was naturalised in 1999, almost a quarter of a century after coming to America.

'For me, part of my gratitude to the American people is to do something about this illegal immigration.'

If Carmen still feels like an outsider in this country, she doesn't show it. She smiles with the confidence of a woman who has found her calling. Her voice overflows with the positive energy of gratitude and born-again patriotism. There is no rage when she talks, no audible resentment.

'This is still a wonderful country. I know. I work with patriots every day.'

Carmen's destination is a ridge overlooking the border near an unofficial fence the Minutemen have erected at their own expense. Carmen gets out of the pick-up with her binoculars in her hand and her Colt .45 hanging from her hip. She stares down the ugly gash ripping through the verdant desert foliage which separates the United States from Mexico.

'This is where we did our first operation, right here on this very line. We stayed here for thirty days and got incredible attention.'

She is smiling wistfully as if the memory of a childhood romance has just popped into her head.

'It's been a battle, but a rewarding battle.'

The battle began just after 9/11 when Carmen and another Tombstone businessman founded a neighbourhood watch group to beef up border security.

'All of a sudden people realised what was happening. We realised how many people were breaking into this country.'

Within a couple of years, Carmen's group had 400 members. They eventually became the Minutemen and membership soared to 9,000. As her volunteers spread out across the border with their lawnchairs and binoculars, Carmen became involved in lobbying against an immigration reform bill which would have given illegal immigrants a path to amnesty. She spent five weeks in Washington with a coalition of conservative and anti-immigrant groups successfully campaigning for its defeat.

Carmen doesn't have the same bipolar quality you often notice in right-wing activists, that same low specific heat moving from instant boil to sudden freeze. Perhaps it is the Teutonic blood in her veins which allows her to express her thoughts in a steady, temperate tone. Yet when when you try to pin down the impulses that motivate her, a slight chill creeps into the conversation.

Carmen doesn't spend a lot of time making the economic argument against immigration; there are no angry declarations that Mexicans are taking American jobs. Instead, the images of 9/11 persist. Carmen sees illegal immigration as part of a broader attack on the United States, not just on its borders but on its way of life.

'When people came to Ellis Island, they were registered.

I believe this wave of immigration is different. Because they sneak in illegally, I believe they will not respect our laws and will not respect the traditions that made this country.'

Carmen's even-tempered veneer hides something darker. She begins to speak with disturbing certainty about tales of sickness and disease. For example, she says, the growing use of pacemakers is linked to an illness carried by immigrants: 'I waited two years to become a citizen. I went through a thorough health check and, believe you me, none of these illegals have gone through these checks. We have diseases entering this country again which are very deadly. We have strains of TB which can't be treated with a simple antibiotic. We have parasites that enter the person's heart and kill them. I have five grandkids and I am very passionate about health, so these isues are very important to me.'

And as we stare at the border in the late afternoon sun, we travel through Carmen's deepest fears, from pandemic all the way through to terrorism.

'We know that al-Qaeda members have been stopped trying to get into this country, so the threat is there, absolutely.'

Looking towards that border, that straight line through the dirt, it becomes clear what it must look like to Carmen. It is a vortex spewing out all the evil that threatens her idealised version of America. On the other side, there is dark matter waiting to assume human shape and burrow its way into the very foundations of the shining city. Carmen spent her whole life searching for her sanctuary. She cannot bear to see her dream soiled, contaminated, by the sum of all her fears. And so she stands there on the frontier, waving her arms, flying a flag, making enough noise to attract the attention of a slumbering city behind her.

A helicopter comes out of nowhere. A flash of blue and white passing over Carmen's silver Chevy, following that dirt-brown gash in the desert. As she stares into her binoculars like a jumpy sentry, an ambulance drives by, kicking up a cloud of dirt and filling it with luminous red and blue lights. There is no siren, which suggests that this is not yet an emergency. There may still be time to find out what's going on.

At an even speed, Carmen follows the straight line of the border until she sees the helicopter resting in a clearing beside the ambulance and a vehicle with the green and white livery of the official Border Patrol. The aircraft's rotors are still turning quickly, but there is no sign of activity.

Carmen gets out of her pick-up and saunters into the brush to find someone to talk to but returns within a couple of minutes.

'I don't know what's happening. He's not telling me. We found a water bottle, so it must involve illegal aliens.'

The helicopter has started to shift slightly on the ground and within seconds it jerks skyward, falling into a broad sweeping turn away from the border and towards the thick desert vegetation. The pilot is looking for something, or someone.

Carmen has no more fearful stories to tell now. She speaks with some sympathy about the plights of the individuals she wants to keep out of her country, about those exploited by the human smugglers, the coyotes.

'They are dropped here by the coyotes and told that Tucson is over the hill. But it's still 120 miles away and all they have with them is a half-bottle of water.'

When she is asked for a specific case which might illustrate the dangers, her eyes seem to flicker a little as if she is running through a rolling index of horror.

'Our group has found a lot of dead bodies. Just recently we came across a couple. The man was an amputee. He had been left wandering for days and had blisters on the stump where his prosthesis used to be.'

It is not the savagery of the image which shocks most. It is the coexistence of compassion and fear in Carmen's monologue.

173

She and her volunteers see such evil in that border: they imagine mortal danger in those who cross it; they rage against the politicians who will not build a wall to keep them out. And yet at the very same time, they see themselves as saviours, both of a nation's integrity and the lives of those who would soil it.

'We always carry water and food and have saved about 350 lives.'

There is that wistful smile on Carmen's face again, as if such acts of humanity help the Minutemen as much as the illegals.

'This is the rewarding part. When you can help save lives.'

—•—

About 100 miles west of Tombstone, just south of Tucson, the hard tarmac has just given way to the soft sand of a desert track. As far as the eye will take you there are creosote bushes and saguaro and cholla cacti pushing all the way to the shimmering outline of mountains and, presumably, to Mexico.

At the wheel of the heavy blue truck is Pastor Robin Hoover, singing slowly to himself to the tune of 'Rawhide': 'Rollin' Rollin' Rollin' … boy, my ass is swollen.'

He is that kind of man of God, profane and passionate. In spite of his rough mouth and his simple workshirt and baseball cap, the Pastor carries himself with pride and distinction. As we bounce over the pockmarked track, he leans forward on the steering wheel until his pale beard and dark glasses are almost touching the windscreen.

'I'm looking for the station, which should be right around … .'

He leans back with resignation on his face.

'Somebody has obviously taken the flag down.'

Pastor Robin Hoover is the founder of and guiding light for an organisation called Humane Borders, which maintains a network of emergency water-stations in the desert. Each station contains two 58-gallon drums of water and has a blue flag on a thirty-foot pole to indicate its position. They are dotted along Arizona's Avara Valley, which leads all the way to the Mexican city of Altar, the main staging-post for people trying to cross the border. 'More people will successfully cross through this valley every year,' says the Pastor, 'than live in the city of Tucson, which has over 600,000 people.' This desolate, scorched stretch of desert is what the Pastor calls the 'Grand Central Station' of migration.

The Pastor pulls his vehicle to a stop on the soft verge of the desert track and leans towards the passenger window to get a better look.

'Ha, ha, ha …' He laughs with emphatic bitterness and then says in a rough, Texan accent: 'It's gone.'

The Pastor gets out and unlocks the back of his blue truck where he keeps the replacement equipment.

'There's another station up here a couple of miles and I think we are going to experience the same thing. It's hunting season so we've had hundreds of people through here in the last couple of days.'

There is nothing where the water station used to be except for the word 'bitches', which the vandals have scrawled in the sand. The Pastor chooses not to dwell on the destruction, and with another volunteer called Paul he unloads two empty water drums and starts to draw the hose out of the back of the truck to fill them.

'Out here, water is like gold. It is the most valuable commodity there is,' he says. But too many people find that out the hard way. 'Many of these migrants have no knowledge of the desert before they get here. People say they should know better. Well, it's not in their lived experience to be in a place like this, to walk for four hours and not see another human being, or water for that matter.'

The Pastor holds the metal-tipped head of the hose a few inches from the mouth of the barrel and a dappled column of water flows through the plastic opening. Humane Borders supplies 30,000 gallons of water to undocumented immigrants trekking through the Avara Valley every year.

'Every day between January and May, 6,500 people begin a trek into Arizona alone. During the summer, the number falls to 600 but that is when most of the water is drunk. That is when someone dies out here every day.'

The Pastor says that back in 1995 there were no recorded deaths on the Arizona border, but in 2007 300 people will die crossing the frontier. They are victims of an immigration policy that seems to lurch back and forth like a punch-drunk boxer, pummelled from one side by angry appeals for a crack-down and clobbered from another by the impossible demands of a vast, porous border.

Back in the 1990s, the authorities came up with a compromise: they would pour all their resources into a blockade of illegal crossings in Texas and California. That would solve the bigger problem, since no one would be foolish enough to try to cross through the hellish conditions of Arizona's Sonora Desert, where temperatures can reach 50 degrees celsius during summer days and fall far below freezing on winter nights. But they obviously didn't understand the coyotes. The smuggler gangs switched routes and began to channel hundreds of thousands of men, women and children across the Arizona frontier. The result is that 3,100 people have died along this stretch of border country since 1998.

Looking back, the authorities either dangerously under-estimated the desperation that drives the migrants or wilfully decided to raise the price of admission to America. Pastor Hoover pulls no punches when he describes the surge of migration through his valley. 'They have been pushed here by the policies of law enforcement,' he says. 'Policy-makers have deliberately chosen tactics that will lead to the death of many migrants.'

The official figures speak of a quiet carnage. The Government Accountability Office has said the number of migrants who died crossing the US border with Mexico reached a high of 472 in 2005. But in Pima County, which includes the Tucson area, the death toll continues to rise. The county's medical examiner dealt with the deaths of 177 people crossing the border in the first eight months of 2007, more than the same period in 2005. His office spends up to $200,000 every year and deploys ten staff to care for and identify the bodies of those who die. In the summer of 2005, there were so many bodies they had to buy an 18-wheeler truck to store them. Since then, the county has built a refrigerated mortuary.

Pastor Hoover spends a lot of the time talking in cold figures but occasionally there is a searing flash of anger. 'This is a phenomenal human tragedy,' he says with feeling. 'These are not numbers; they are human beings.'

The Pastor founded Humane Borders back in 2000 out of the church that he runs in Tucson. There had been a rash of migrant deaths in the desert outside town and the Pastor was moved in particular by the story of one young woman who gave her last water to her infant child. She died but her child survived.

Now Humane Borders has more than 63 trained drivers and 8,000 volunteers who maintain 87 water stations on both sides of the border. The group distributes maps in Mexico and Central America that show the location of water stations and emergency beacons. It also marks the sites of migrant deaths and carries a warning: 'Don't do it. There's not enough water. Don't pay the penalty.'

Ultimately, the group is driven forward by the potent technicolour personality of Pastor Robin Hoover. He is perfectly suited to the savagery of this hidden border war. He grew up in the west Texas town of Big Spring and is full of the contradictions that shape that harsh corner of America. On the one hand, he is a plain-spoken working man who has held jobs in nursing, photography, and construction. But he is also a social activist; before he moved to Tucson, he ministered to border communities in the Rio Grande Valley. At the very same time, he is an uncompromising intellectual with three university degrees, including a doctorate in political science.

He is both hero and villian, and seems to enjoys both personae. He speaks with pride about the Human Rights award he received from the Mexican President Felipe Calderón. But he also seems to draw energy from the hatred directed his way by the Minutemen, who accuse him of 'sedition' and 'aiding and abetting criminal activity'.

There is a touch of the bare-knuckle bruiser about him. You quickly realise it is very easy to get on his wrong side, which is a cold and scary place. 'I'm a religious man but I am not a pious man,' he says, steering his truck through the desert. 'I will call a chicken fucker a chicken fucker.' He grew up just a half-hour's drive from George W. Bush's hometown of Midland, but he is a million miles from its narrow conservatism. 'Bush is all west Texas,' he says. 'There is no blood in him.'

Language is clearly important to Pastor Hoover. He prefers to call the phenomenal surge of people across that border 'migration' rather than 'immigration'. He refuses to use the word 'illegal' to describe the people who cross. And when it comes to his views of the Minutemen, he resists the urge to utter obscenities and chooses to call them 'vigilantes of fear'.

The Pastor accepts that the trigger for the current wave of anti-immigrant sentiment in America was 9/11, but he has no time for the powerful existential vulnerability that came with it. Instead, he chooses to focus on the Machiavellian urge of leaders who manipulated the surge of nationalism that followed the attack on the Twin Towers.

'This is a resistance fuelled by cultural imperialism. But, more importantly, it is being fuelled by politicians who feel that anti-migrant sentiment is good for their electoral prospects.'

While you don't hear much talk of economics from Carmen Mercer, the Pastor believes that people like her are searching for scapegoats at a time of increasing uncertainty. They blame the migrants from Mexico without even understanding who they are. 'These are not just the poorest of the poor,' he says. 'Not all of them come for low-wage jobs. These are people making a significant contribution to our economy.'

Look at the border through the eyes of Pastor Robin Hoover and you see that it offers no protection. It is an impediment, it a blockage in an otherwise healthy artery, bringing nothing but pain to the heart of American life.

'If you want to increase national security, if you are worried by the illegal side of it, just give them a visa.'

It took the Pastor a single step to get to that conclusion. He has little time for anyone who can't make the same leap of faith, especially the likes of Carmen Mercer.

'There are people who come down here and sit on their lawn-chairs and strap on their .45s and talk big. They have been run over by globalisation and don't know what else to do.'

—•—

Carmen Mercer has her video camera held just far enough from her face so that she can see the screen sticking out from the side. She is well pleased with what she sees.

'It seems like it is double panels and they are very tight together. Very effective.'

Carmen sounds like a teacher praising a model student. She walks towards the new stretch of government-built fence, holding her camera as she goes, providing a running commentary.

'And I would say it is almost 15 feet high also.'

The fence is made up of tall black plastic poles and narrow mesh. It looks fragile but not to Carmen.

'That's concrete at the base, so they can't dig underneath, so it's, eh ... a good construction.'

The evening sun warms Carmen's face. She looks as if she is close to tears. The new stretch of wall will run for 30 miles of that 2000-mile-long frontier.

'I am glad to see it ... finally happening. Absolutely.'

—•—

E pluribus unum. It is the most important phrase in the American lexicon: out of many, one. You'll find the phrase on the dollar bill and the humble cent as a gentle reminder to the common people of the United States that there is strength in difference. But it is also a warning that without a regular transfusion of fresh blood, America would not be America.

Immigration brings constant renewal but also the clash of opposites which makes the US such an unnerving spectacle. To better understand the American experience of immigration, it helps to revisit our hidden code, that tension between Frontier and Ritual. To become American, the immigrants must play the role of pioneers and make the journey across the frontier. Once safely across, they must immerse themselves in the rituals which transform a foreigner into an American, a pioneer into a settler. But at both stages of this process there are recurring problems with each successive wave of immigration. The first point of conflict is described best by Andro Linklater in *The Fabric of America*. He sums up American history as a dynamic and difficult interaction between 'those already inside the frontier who naturally wish to preserve what is there, and those who want to cross the frontier and will inevitably alter the existing state of things'.

The second recurring battle arises from the impact of immigration on the rituals that form the American identity. By its very nature, immigration is a process of creative destruction in which old rituals are pushed aside in favour of new ones. What strikes one observer as a fine blend of cultures will look like an unappetising mess to another. Irish poet and songwriter Thomas Moore visited the United States in the early years of the nineteenth century and was repelled by what he saw:

Tis one dull chaos, one unfertile strife
Betwixt half-polish'd and half-barbarous life;
Where every ill the ancient world could brew
Is mix'd with every grossness of the new.

If that is what the melting pot looks like to an outsider, what does it feel like to be up to your neck in its slow simmer? According to historian Michael Kammen, Americans have always 'vacillated between self-praise for being a nation of immigrants and self-hate for the stations of restless locomotion through which we daily pass'.

The self-hate has been most intense during the three great waves of immigration that have changed American history, in the 1850s, 1880s and early years of the 20th century. That first great wave is the one which we in Ireland will be most familiar with, since it coincides with our own post-Famine exodus. Historians record the first mention of immigration as a source of party political controversy in 1848, and within a few years, America has its first explicitly anti-immigrant movement, the Know Nothings.

By the end of 1854, two million Irish had arrived in the United States and many more were to follow. In 1856, the Know Nothing candidate, Millard Fillmore, won more than a fifth of all the votes cast in that year's presidential election. Anti-immigrant forces were so strong that it looked as if they might take control of the emerging Republican Party. But in the end, the Republicans became the party of Abraham Lincoln and other, more pressing issues, like civil war, removed immigration from

181

the political agenda. This cycle seems to repeat itself with each successive wave of immigration. A surge in new arrivals triggers a rise in anti-immigrant sentiment. The panic eventually peaks and then wanes, while the new immigrants settle down and change America for the better.

What we are witnessing today is a fourth great wave of immigration surging onto American shores. The US Census Bureau calculates that one American is born every seven seconds, one dies every 13 seconds, and an immigrant arrives every 31 seconds. America is expected to add another 100 million to its population during the next forty years and a growing share of the new citizens will have been born somewhere else. Back in 1970, new immigrants accounted for five per cent of the US population. Today, it is 12 per cent and rising; if trends continue, there will be a record-breaking proportion of foreign-born Americans by 2025.

These figures alone point to a literal reinvention of the United States. But there is also the possibility that change could be retarded by the anti-immigrant sentiment bubbling away in Arizona and beyond. History tells us that this period of nativist panic will eventually tire itself out, and those new immigrants will quietly renew and refresh the American identity. But after spending time with Carmen Mercer and Pastor Hoover, you have to ask if we can we safely make that assumption.

There are clear parallels between the current conflict over immigration and what has come before. It is still a conflict between those who guard the frontier and those who wish to pass it, between those who wish to preserve American rituals and those bound to change them. But we need to be mindful of what is dangerously unique about the conflict we are witnessing on that border.

To begin with, the war of words over immigration is enmeshed in a far wider struggle. This wave of new migrants began arriving at the tail-end of the 'culture war' for control of

America's identity, fought between liberals and conservatives. Immigration is just another flash-point between two very different world views which emerged from the convulsions of the 1960s. One one side are the liberal, educated cosmopolitans who, in the words of commentator David Brooks, 'valued diversity and embraced a sense of national identity that rested on openness and global integration'. Out of this group came the Moses generation, about which Barack Obama spoke, the pioneers who pushed back the frontiers of social and racial justice, who fought to tame the uncivilised instincts of the American psyche. Their high ideals are still reflected in the uncompromising principles of Pastor Robin Hoover.

But their challenge to the established order created a backlash among those who valued American rituals as they were, who placed community above the individual, tradition above change. 'Members of this class came to feel that America's identity and culture were under threat,' writes David Brooks, 'from people who didn't understand what made America united and distinct'. Today, you will feel the hard edge of that backlash on the US–Mexican border. You will hear it in Carmen Mercer's fearful rhetoric and see it in human form resting on a lawnchair with a Colt .45.

The culture war absorbs many different debates into a single, all-encompassing clash of opposing world views. That tends to strengthen the hand of the immigration zealots. Hardliners on that border would have far less sway were they not symbols of the broader resistance against a cosmopolitan elite who do not understand the real America. Carmen Mercer is the antidote to those urban liberals who look beyond their big cities and see nothing but rednecks, blue collars and white trash.

The traditionalists feel besieged by the liberals and so tend to make simplistic judgements about them. They ignore the fact that among the agents of change are God-fearing, small-town Americans like Pastor Robin Hoover. But, at the very same time, open-minded and educated men like the Pastor can be brutally dismissive of those who disagree with them. Granted, there is not a lot of room for nuance in a life and death struggle like this, but too few people with the Pastor's views seem to have more than a partial understanding of the fear which drives decent people, as well as zealots, to resist immigration.

The Minutemen occupy the political fringe, but many Americans will accept the central premise of their argument: that America is a rare elixir to be shared out among those who play by the rules. If this scarce treasure is to be offered to newcomers, it must happen gradually, carefully. Any sudden uncontrolled influx of people and that American elixir is diluted and weakened for ever. This very same visceral fear has ebbed and flowed through American history. During each great wave of immigration, Americans face the same challenge and ultimately, sometimes reluctantly, pass the same test. They eventually come to see the truth in those words: *E pluribus unum*.

But Carmen Mercer says this time it's different. What is happening on the southwest frontier of the United States has no parallel in American history. In at least one sense, she is right. The life of an immigrant had far more value when the Irish were flocking to America more than a century ago. You certainly won't find an Ellis Island anywhere along the 2,000 miles of frontier with Mexico. There will be no memorials and statues at those staging points for the illegals, no statues to commemorate the thousands who never made it along the way. They once used an old pioneer motto to describe new arrivals on American shores: 'The cowards never started and the weak died on the way.' They would not dare use it now.

Of course, this is not the difference that Carmen had in mind. What she would like Americans to focus on is the fact that the fourth wave of immigration is predominantly from one source: Latin America. Unlike the broad range of nationalities and cultures represented in previous waves of immigration,

Spanish-speakers dominate this wave, with Latinos expected to make up one quarter of the US population by 2050. If the anti-immigrant activist has two favourite facts, it is that salsa replaced ketchup as the most popular condiment in America right about the time Jose became the most popular name in California and Texas.

Previous waves of migrants came from far across the sea, not from next door. Traditionalist academics like Samuel Huntington note that the income gap between the US and Mexico is the largest between any two adjoining countries in the world. This creates the perfect condition for a long-term invasion of migrants from 'a poor contiguous country, with more than a third of the population of the United States, who come across a two-thousand-mile border marked historically simply by a line in the ground and a shallow river.'

The critics say that another distinguishing feature of this wave of new arrivals is the number of 'illegals' among them. By one estimate, the number of undocumented immigrants grew by 770,000 per year in the 1990s, and they will keep coming at a rate of more than half a million for the rest of this decade. You could argue that the biggest danger here is that illegal immigrants will be trapped in the shadows of American life, never having the chance to truly assimilate as others have done before them.

Without assimilation, immigration is a force for division, not renewal. In his book *Who Are We?*, Samuel Huntington argues that the current wave of Latino immigrants are proving hard to integrate into American life, partly because they are more likely to retain citizenship of their country of origin. 'With dual citizenship, American identity is no longer distinctive and exceptional,' Huntington writes. 'American citizenship becomes simply an add-on to another citizenship.'

Huntington and other traditionalists rely heavily on statistics that suggest that Spanish-speaking new arrivals from Latin America are slower to integrate than other kinds of immigrants, statistics that prove that this wave of immigration is different, presumably more dangerous. They provide an authoritative voice to the guttural fears of people in lawnchairs on that broken border. But there is a weakness in their perspective, a failure to appreciate the growing importance of immigration in America's developing transformation.

In the first place, the critics of immigration suffer from what demographer Dowell Myers calls the 'Peter Pan Fallacy'. They seem fixated on only the very latest arrivals and assume that all immigrants remain 'forever frozen in their status as new-comers, never aging, never advancing economically, and never assimilating'. Here's how they fall victim to the fallacy: they focus on the fact that just a third of Latino immigrants who have been in America for less than ten years speak English well. But they seem to ignore the long-term trend and the fact that nine of out ten children of immigrants speak the language well and the figure rises to 97 per cent among their grandchildren.

Previous waves of immigrants did integrate more quickly, mainly because more of them had English as a first language, but the long-term trends for this batch of new arrivals are encouraging. In May 2008, the Manhattan Institute published a report showing that the rate of assimilation has substantially quickened in recent decades. The report found that even the newest arrivals, the Peter Pans, were merging into American life at a faster pace than the traditionalists had imagined.

Perhaps the greatest mistake the traditionalists make is to assume that they continue to speak for the majority of Americans on immigration. To be fair, they could be forgiven for thinking that they do. After all, like-minded politicians killed off proposals to reform the immigration system, and hardline positions on immigration played well in the early stage of the 2008 presidential campaign. When it comes to public opinion, a CBS News poll in 2007 found that 69 per cent of people wanted illegal immigrants deported.

But the same poll revealed an interesting ambivalence about immigration among Americans – a love–hate relationship that may be tilting slightly towards grudging affection. When people were offered an alternative to deportation for illegal immigrants who had been in American for more than two years, 62 per cent took it. The poll also found a declining hostility to immigrants, 57 per cent saying that most recent immigrants contributed to the United States (up 23 points from 1986) and just 28 per cent saying that most immigrants caused problems (a drop of 16 per cent).

Another telling expression of (conservative) public opinion was the nomination of John McCain, the Republican who annoys the anti-immigration lobby most.

The fourth great wave of immigration is not yet over, but it seems that the usual rise in anti-immigrant sentiment may have passed its peak. There is just one remaining cloud on the horizon, and that is the apparent weakness of the American economy. If economic insecurity is the driving force behind anti-immigrant sentiment, then you would expect a renewed surge of resistance during a recession. And what if the United States were entering a period of long-term stagnation? What if immigration no longer promised renewal but was seen as an added burden on a nation in decline?

The omens do not seem good. The United States has borrowed, spent and imported far beyond its means. Its financial system is teetering under the weight of the sub-prime fiasco and is beginning to face stiff competition from surging economies like China and India. And yet there are good reasons to believe that rumours of America's demise have been greatly exaggerated.

Here's the delicious irony: the very thing that will save the United States from the bitter wages of economic decline is immigration. What you often forget as you listen to all the angry talk about a broken border, is that the US has successfully absorbed more than 20 million legal immigrants over the past quarter-century. No other country has ever enjoyed such an invigorating injection of human capital.

Just think of the advantages this surge in population will give the United States. While other countries get older and less productive, America will be kept vibrant and youthful by rising fertility and surging immigration. In 2050, the average American will be under 40, while the average European and Japanese will be more than a decade older. And what of China, America's greatest potential rival? Its median age will rise from 33 in 2005 to 45 in 2050. While other countries are getting more pensioners, the US will be creating more workers.

A younger, more dynamic society is also a more innovative society. The US economy is expected create one million new high-tech jobs over the next decade, mainly because America continues to be the home of invention and reinvention. The World Economic Forum continues to rate the United States first in technology and innovation, first in spending for research and technology and first in the quality of its research institutions. The US produces one-third of the world's scientific papers, employs two-thirds of the world's Nobel prizewinners, has seven or eight of the world's top ten universities (depending on which ranking you choose) and leads the world in the education of computer scientists.

And guess what? Immigration will keep the United States on the cutting edge. It spends more than twice as much on higher education than Europe, which helps it to attract 30 per cent of students around the world who study in another country. Foreign students and immigrants do remarkably well once they arrive in the US, getting 65 per cent of all computer science PhDs awarded by American colleges. Once they graduate, these tech-savvy immigrants tend to put down roots: half of all start-up companies in Silicon Valley had at least one founder who was foreign-born.

It is hard to argue with Fareed Zakaria of *Newsweek* when he says '…the United States' potential new burst of productivity, its edge in nano technology and biotechnology, its ability to invent the future – all rest on its immigration policies.' In other words, the unfolding transformation of the United States cannot be sustained unless the new arrivals keep coming in overwhelming, invigorating numbers. Of course, native-born Americans must find a way of coping with the upheaval that brings.

The challenge is to find common purpose on immigration, to overcome both the paranoid and the legitimate fears that come with millions of new arrivals. An important first step will be an end to that 'culture war'. As long as America is divided into tribes of zealous traditionalists and hard-edged idealists, you struggle to see how there can be a rational debate about broken borders or the problems of integration. The rise of the Joshua generation is the best hope of ending tribal political warfare. But that would be a first step, not a final solution. Ultimately, it all comes down to that age-old tension between Frontier and Ritual.

So far, we have discovered that the reinvention of America involves a decisive shift towards Ritual and the rise of a new civic and collective ethic. But some elements of transformation require Americans to rediscover Frontier. Immigration is one of them. It demands the qualities of innovation and change, dislocation and danger, which energised the original pioneers. After all, it is that dangerous, dynamic frontier ethic which keeps the immigrants coming, which keeps renewing America. The words *E pluribus unum* sit on the Frontier side of the equation.

But this is a hard sell in an era of doubt. Ritual is a safe place to be when times get hard. One of the most difficult parts of America's reinvention is persuading the born-again patriots, the struggling blue-collar workers and the pious young boomburb families that they should embrace reinvention and all the creative destruction it involves.

At certain moments in their history, Americans have risen to the challenge and confronted their problems head-on. At others, they have retreated behind the walls of their 'city on the hill' to find sanctuary. These competing instincts are at work in that angry conflict over immigration, but they are also shaping a fearful debate about America's wider role in global affairs. Which brings us to our last big question: how do you reinvent a nation that fears the world as much as the world fears it?

9.

Titan – The Boomburb Empire

'This was ground zero for at least one missile.'

When our guide, Harry, says these words, he finally sounds as if he has a soul. We all breathe a little easier, even though he's talking about nuclear holocaust.

Harry has spent the last 20 minutes describing the features of this former Titan II missile base as if he were an affable salesman in a suburban car showroom pointing out the finer points of fuel efficiency, anti-lock brakes and skid-control.

Under a corrugated metal roof, he showed our tour group the engine that would have sent the 103-foot missile on its 6,000-mile journey towards the Apocalypse. He told us that it would have powered up for just five minutes of the 35-minute flight to the Soviet Union. The rest of the trip would have been an intercontinental glide. He also gave an intricate explanation of the composition of the coolant agent and the boiling point of the propellant, or maybe it was the other way round. Memory is an unreliable guide at this point; it was impossible not to be distracted by the fact that Harry's white hard-hat was the same colour as his shorts and his blue polo shirt matched the socks around his ankles.

But now, as we stand right by the half-open silo roof, we are gripped by each and every word he utters. Harry has just pointed out that on Doomsday, the Soviets would have surely chosen this flat, featureless piece of Arizona desert, just over the ridge from the small town of Sahuarita, as a target for nuclear attack.

For the first time, this no longer feels like a museum; it is the front line of the Cold War at the moment of its potentially catastrophic climax. With a few words, Harry has transported us back to the early 1960s. This is now one of 18 active missile bases dotted along the outer edges of Tucson, Arizona. Inside the single silo, on the tip of that missile, is the largest nuclear device ever deployed by the United States: a nine-megaton W-53 warhead with the explosive power of six hundred Hiroshimas. The warhead is designed to detonate either as a 'groundburst', which would take out a reinforced military target, or an 'airburst', which would have annihilated a Soviet city. If and when Doomsday arrives, our warhead will explode in a groundburst. The news brings with it a disorienting jolt of relief.

From the outset of the tour, the guides at the Titan Missile Museum had encouraged us to look for shades of grey in the black and white reality of Mutually Assured Destruction. The museum does not simply illustrate history, it also provides an explanation, occasionally even a justification. Before we left on our hour-long tour with Harry, we were shown a video in the briefing room presented by the museum's archivist, Chuck Penson. With his long ponytail and nerdy charm, he was an unlikely but compelling spokesman for the doctrine of 'peace through deterrence'. Penson played the role of a US Air Force 'missileer' arriving at the command bunker for a 24-hour shift, picking up the chunky, old telephone receiver and reading the secret code that will gain him entry. As he turned back to the camera to explain the base's security procedures, he pulled a lighter out of his pocket and set fire to the piece of paper carrying the code he had just read. Having hooked us with his amateur dramatics, Chuck delivered the punchline, telling us that 'peace isn't won. It is kept, from moment to moment.'

Penson's troubling logic stays with us as we finally get our chance to descend into the command bunker. But it is not half as disturbing as the sign at the bottom of the first set of stairs warning us to look out for rattlesnakes. Harry explains that serpents occasionally seek refuge from the unforgiving desert heat on the cool, shaded concrete at the entrance to the bunker.

There are just 55 steps between ground level and the door of the command post. That doesn't put a lot of distance between us and the thermo-nuclear fireball that may be about to consume this corner of Arizona. But Harry is waiting there with another thick sliver of comfort: a four-foot-thick steel door which he has manfully wrenched open.

He explains that almost everything in the bunker is mounted on springs, from the light fixtures to the missile itself. This would protect us from blast waves, assuming those crazy Soviet bastards dropped the big one on Sahuarita first (these are not Harry's exact words but you must realise we are emotionally invested in his tour at this point).

We are finally led to the control room, which is a minimalist copy of the bridge of the Starship *Enterprise*. If this really were 1962, the walls of blinking lights, the surgical green steel panelling and the rows of buttons and keys on the commander's console would be unbearably futuristic. But in 2008, it's amusingly retro. The spell is broken, momentarily.

Harry is off again, talking about gizmos and gadgets, and the members of the group are now furtively checking each other out. In the close proximity of the control room, it becomes apparent just how diverse the people on this tour are. We are in the middle of a scary movie surrounded by the comforting faces of everyday America. A black father has brought his two kids. One of them is an adorable young boy, not much older than seven or eight, whom Harry invites to sit in the commander's grey plastic chair.

Right behind are two contrasting couples. One young man and woman look suspiciously like honeymooners, all tactile gestures and private jokes. Sitting on a bench beside them are an elderly couple. The husband is a former military man, a sergeant. We know this because his wife asks a question which turns into a bitter complaint about the treatment of young servicemen.

Lurking in the back is a refined sixty-something couple who are travelling with their adult son. He has a hipster's light scraggly beard and is wearing a flat cap, long camouflage shorts and a T-shirt advertising the attractions of San Francisco. He seems ill at ease and holds his big camera close to his side, loaded and ready to use.

Harry returns to the juicy detail. He is about to explain the launch procedure. A charge of nervous excitement runs through the room, but some of us also have a hint of something bitter on our tongues. It tastes of revulsion.

Before Harry begins, he points out the warning stenciled in big red letters on the walls at various points around the command bunker: 'No lone zone. Two man policy mandatory.' During their 24-hour shift (and presumably the duration of the Apocalypse) the two missileers on duty would do virtually everything in plain sight of each either, just in case one of them went whack-a-doodle.

Harry points to the red safe in the corner of the control room which contained the codes that would have had to be verified before the launch. Then he tells us he will need an assistant; after all, this is a 'no lone zone'. Before anyone has a chance to volunteer, Harry picks the little boy sitting in the commander's seat. He points to the keys sitting in the two consoles and explains that both missileers would have to insert their keys at the very same moment and turn them simultaneously to initiate the launch sequence.

Harry and the young boy turn their keys together. Now it's intimate all over again. That bitter taste is getting stronger. The room is on edge despite the calm, mechanical tone in Harry's voice. We try to keep up with it but his words are a jumble. An alarm bell goes off without warning. Feet leave the ground.

Blood drains. Harry smiles. His understated presence gives us more room to ponder the terrifying potential of the clinical routine we are witnessing.

It takes 58 seconds from the moment the keys are inserted to the moment that the Titan missile starts to climb out of the silo.

There are loose ends that we would have liked to clear up before we sent our missile on its way. Do we know the actual location of the target? Does it have a name? Can we see it on a map? What value does it have as a target? What was the purpose of destroying it? Why there?

You can see how easily you would tie yourself in knots with that kind of thinking. The clear imperative in this bunker was to execute one routine after another. Worry about the daily grind of a 24-hour-shift. You are a soldier. A technician. Just do your damn job like the professional you are and let someone above your pay grade do the deep thinking.

Still, it would have been very hard not to think deep mortal thoughts. We passed through that four-foot steel door but are still worried about the odds of survival down here. After all, we are a mere 55 steps from ground zero. For the first time, Harry seems a little sheepish. He admits that the missileers would not have survived an attack by a Soviet nuclear missile if it had landed in close proximity. Even if they had survived the brutal, definitive exchange of missiles, they would have faced an impossible choice. They had enough food to last a month but enough air for only a week or so.

'After ten days,' Harry says, 'they would have a choice whether to suffocate down here or go back up and face that new world.'

It is time we saw that missile, if only to make sure it is still in place and the world is as we left it a few minutes ago. Harry leads us down a long, bright corridor and warns the taller gentleman among us to watch out for the low roof. The corridor ends at a half-open green metal door with the red-stencil 'lone zone' warning on it. Behind it, two mannequins in space suits strike a pose as if filling the rocket with something (it's either propellant or coolant, but we dare not ask).

As we inch closer and Harry begins talking about the shock-absorbing tiles around the walls of the silo, the eye is drawn to the gentle patterns on the panels of the mid-section of the missile. The rivets run in a pointed arc across the copper surface like the windows of a medieval Arabian citadel. Perhaps not everyone will see the resemblance.

Harry encourages us to spread out and take advantage of the glass windows that wrap around the circular girth of the Titan. After the twilight of the bunker it is a shock to see the torrent of natural desert light flooding down the silo. The roof is permanently half-open, as mandated by the Arms Control Treaties which ended the Titan programme. The Soviets and the Americans wanted to be able to peer into the silos with their satellites to make sure that they remain decommissioned.

The vaguely Islamic design of the missile's mid-section is countered by the shape of the top of the missile, which brings to mind a copper-clad church steeple before it is ravaged by the rain and wind. It seems natural to be in a religious frame of mind as we stare at that tower of awesome destruction. After all, we are standing in front of mankind's best effort yet to appropriate the vengeful wrath of God.

Harry is coming to the end of his time with us. There are a few questions still to be asked but none that an ordinary mortal, even one so genial and accomplished as Harry, could answer to anyone's satisfaction.

We shall take those questions with us as we go back up the stairs into the dry heat, and retreat to the gift shop, where we peel away wordlessly from the group and become individuals again, stirred, if not shaken.

Just a few hundred yards from the main gate of the museum is a familiar cluster of light-brown stucco homes, a sign for a golf club and then an upmarket trailerpark. While we were down in that bunker, the suburbs crept south along route 19 past Tucson airport all the way up to the gates of the Apocalypse.

If you are a glass half-full type of person, you will draw comfort from this. Weapons of global destruction are becoming just another suburban attraction, wedged between the water park and the new Circuit City. The days of the Evil Empire are over. Welcome to life in the Boomburb Empire. This is a comforting thought: odd, but comforting.

Yet that hour in the bunker is a disturbing reminder that America's greatest contradictions outlived the Cold War: the United States was created to spread the values of liberty, justice and equality. But to defend its land and promote its values it has resorted to destructive power on a scale without parallel in history. Americans are full of ambition for the world and yet they seem so frightened by it.

The ring of nuclear weaponry surrounding Tucson was designed to keep the young men of the American heartland from fighting other people's wars in distant lands. It offered the United States a chance to shape the world without leaving its shores. It was the riskiest game of roulette ever played, and many Americans clearly believe the gamble paid off.

The doctrine of 'peace through deterrence' is an exhibit in a museum, but its combination of fear and idealism, risk and safety, belief and delusion still battle for the soul of America. The tension between Frontier and Ritual has always shaped America foreign policy. It still does today, even in this era of reinvention.

—•—

Back when the United States was a lovable, snotty-nosed cherub of a nation, George Washington described it as an 'infant empire'. And if Washington was to be the emperor, he resolved to follow the lead of the great Roman consul Lucius Quinctius

Cincinnatus. Cincinnatus was prevailed upon to leave his farm and take the reins of absolute power during a wartime emergency. He saved the empire, returned power to the Senate and went back to ploughing his fields. Washington wanted much the same thing: win the Revolutionary War, oversee the birth of a Republic and return to a life of farming on his beloved estate at Mount Vernon.

Washington was not the only founding father to be influenced by Cincinnatus. Some of the early American revolutionaries founded the Society of Cincinnati, pledging to defend the 'exalted rights and liberties of human nature' and the 'future dignity of the American empire.'

This early cult of Cincinnatus contains the seeds of Frontier and Ritual. Like a later generation of pioneers, those early patriots sacrificed for the dream of self-reliance and independence. But once they had conquered, they sought to return to the comfort of their homestead.

The tension between Frontier and Ritual, essentially the same duality which defined Cincinnatus, has shaped US foreign policy from Washington to Bush. Each president has struggled to advance America's cause while never straying too far from the collective homestead.

Balancing those competing urges was never going to be easy. US presidents have generally chosen the instinct which suited their time. The early idealists like Thomas Jefferson declared the United States to be an 'empire of liberty'. Isolationists like John Quincy Adams said America 'does not go abroad in search of monsters to destroy'. America tends to drift between these competing poles, allowing Frontier to dominate for a while and then veering back to Ritual. America has been outlaw and sheriff, idealist and isolationist, actor and audience, aggressor and protector.

It is easy to see which role occupied America in its early days of expansion. As the great Irish philosopher Bishop Berkeley put it: 'Westward the course of empire takes its way.' What would begin as an ugly, chaotic rush for land and riches on the Western frontier was given a divine, missionary edge by the Irish-American journalist John L. Sullivan in 1845 when he wrote: 'Our manifest destiny [is] to overspread the continent allotted by Providence for the free development of our yearly multiplying millions.' In that phrase 'manifest destiny' was a doctrine of conquest that would influence American foreign policy directly or indirectly for decades to come.

While this was clearly a Frontier philosophy, it was borne of a familiar longing for Ritual, as a popular song of the era reveals:

> All I want in God's Creation
> Is a pretty little wife and a big plantation
> Way up north in the Cherokee Nation.

President Andrew Jackson led the charge against the Native Americans. President James Polk waged war on Mexico. Polk was responsible for the second-largest expansion of American territory and would have tried to take all of Mexico had it not been for Southern politicians who were afraid of polluting white America with too many Mexicans (if only they could have lived to see the Latino wave of the 21st century).

Manifest Destiny eventually fell out of favour but it was not long before the onset of a second imperial phase. The closing years of the nineteenth century brought the Spanish-American war and the conquest of Cuba, Puerto Rico and Guam. In 1898, President William McKinley launched an attack on the Philippines after going down on bended knee and seeking guidance from God. The resulting war would claim the lives of as many as 250,000 Filipino and 4,000 US troops.

McKinley's successor, Teddy Roosevelt, carried a big stick and talked loudly about America's right to intervene anywhere in Latin America (this was known as the Monroe Doctrine).

His claim that 'aggressive fighting for the right is the noblest sport the world affords' was engraved on a plaque on Donald Rumsfeld's desk a century later.

For all his machismo, Roosevelt realised that an imperial-style foreign policy brought imperial-sized burdens. He came to believe that the war in the Philippines was a mistake, and when confronted with the prospect of intervening in the Dominican Republic, he said he had 'about the same desire to annex it as a gorged boa constrictor might have to swallow a porcupine wrong-end-to'.

After Roosevelt, the appetite for foreign intervention waned, and eventually, an anti-imperial instinct began to assert itself. In truth, it had been there for some time. Abraham Lincoln had been a fierce critic of that first war with Mexico, urging his countrymen to 'put a check upon this lust of dominion'.

The first president to live up to America's founding promise to the world was Woodrow Wilson, who pursued the notion of 'collective security' among a broad family of nations. It was an innovation dismissed as naïve by many European leaders, but it would ultimately become a cornerstone of global diplomacy.

At home, Wilson was bitterly attacked by a powerful isolationist lobby who wanted the United States to return home. But his idealistic vision would eventually be revived by Franklin Delano Roosevelt, who forged consensus around a new foreign policy that was both assertive and anti-imperial. His brand of 'liberal internationalism' used military power to preserve stability, but also sought out partnerships in pursuit of American ideals. This blend of Ritual and Frontier would help to win World War II, rebuild Europe, create global institutions and galvanise Western democracy. This was the America which aspired to be umpire, not empire.

The United States was still capable of throwing its weight around, as it did in South and Central America and Indonesia, and its war in Vietnam brought failure and domestic dissent.

Just as these dirty little battles reminded the US of the folly of empire, the nuclear stand-off with the Soviets limited its capacity to act at will.

By the time the Berlin Wall fell in 1989, the United States was the lynchpin of a global system of law and order, but it was also the global sheriff with more firepower than any nation in the history of the world. By the turn of the 21st century it had over 700 bases in more than 30 countries. It was an anti-imperial empire in search of a purpose.

President Bill Clinton earned a reputation as a global peacemaker, but he did his fair share of fighting, launching military action in the Balkans, Sudan, Iraq, Afghanistan, Haiti and Somalia. His Secretary of State, Madeleine Albright, summed up the administrations approach when she said Americans must be 'authors of the history of our age'.

This was the backdrop against which George W. Bush would enter, stage right. He was a man with little knowledge of the world, but what he knew convinced him that America should mind its own business. He promised humility and said he would not tell other nations 'We do it this way, so should you.' As he told a crowd at the Ronald Reagan library in California in 1999:

> America has never been an empire. Let us reject the
> blinders of isolationism, just as we refuse the crown
> of empire. Let us not dominate others with our
> power – or betray them with our indifference. And
> let us have an American foreign policy that reflects
> American character. The modesty of true strength.
> The humility of real greatness.

A lot more Ritual. A little less Frontier. That was what George Bush promised before the planes hit the Twin Towers.

Too many people talk about 9/11 without appreciating the existential shift it forced on individual Americans. The physical distance between foreign wars and the homestead was erased in an instant. The attacks on New York and Washington ended centuries of free security: a happy accident of geography based on what the historian C. Vann Woodward describes as 'nature's gift of three vast bodies of water interposed between this country and any other power that might constitute a serious menace to its safety.' Like a fast car hitting a wall, America lost that free security in an instant. It was that abrupt breach which Woodward says explains the 'faltering and bewildered way in which America faced its new peril'.

Bewilderment and confusion would soon give way to clarity inside the White House. George Bush abandoned the soft layer of Ritual which helped to get him elected and embraced his tense, edgy Frontier instincts. He also turned to a group of policy-advisers who saw a chance to test a theory. Neo-conservatism was not triggered by 9/11; it was a reaction to the fall of the Berlin Wall. The Neo-Cons believed that the collapse of the Soviet Union gave America an opportunity to reshape the world in the name of freedom and democracy, an opportunity they believed Bill Clinton squandered.

They were not imperialists in the classic sense; they were not driven by a thirst for conquest or dominion. But when they got their chance, they were not afraid of America's imperial potential. The journalist Ron Suskind has written the single most illuminating account of their thinking. 'We're an empire now, and when we act, we create our own reality,' a senior Bush adviser told Suskind in the year after 9/11. 'We're history's actors ... and you, all of you, will be left to just study what we do.'

The world knows exactly what the Neo-Cons did and it will be up to history to deliver the ultimate judgement. But here is the more immediate challenge: predicting America's next uncertain steps in the world. As its people continue to cope with the slow-release shock of 9/11 and the trauma of Iraq, they have turned their back on the Neo-Con experiment. But as they scramble for an alternative, will they opt for the reinvention of their foreign policy? What instinct guides them most right now – Frontier or Ritual?

—•—

It is hard to know what a president with a different personality would have made of the existential shock of 9/11. What if he or she had seen an opportunity? What if he had persuaded Americans that survival depended on a more profound engagement with this new, searingly intimate world? Sentences that begin with the words 'what if …' often end in madness, so no more of that.

Rather than predicting how things could have been, let's see how the American world view has evolved, from the end of the Cold War to now. What is striking about public opinion in the years before George Bush was how much Americans wanted to retreat from the role of global sheriff. In two successive polls in the mid-1990s, just one in eight Americans said they thought the United States should be the single leader of the world.

The more things changed, the more they stayed the same, at least when it came to public opinion. For all the patriotic fervour that followed 9/11, and the initial support for the invasion in Iraq, the American people remained convinced that they should play a limited role in the world. In his inaugural address in January 2005, George Bush told his people: 'The best hope for peace in our world is the expansion of freedom in all the world.' But the following month, an opinion poll found that just 31 per cent of Americans believed that building democracy abroad should be a very important goal of their foreign policy. That figure would fall to 27 per cent in September of the same year.

From time to time, the American people will be led overseas in the name of freedom or security, or both. But they must be mightily inspired, manipulated or threatened before they will rouse themselves from the homestead.

We should never assume that the ambitions of American leaders are the same as the preferences of their people. Fundamentally, ordinary Americans have overwhelming pride in their country but have no interest in forcing others to live like them. Most tend to assume that when people are truly free they will choose to live the American way. In the meantime, their default position towards the world is indifference.

A nation that celebrates self-reliance has a hard time working out why others would rely on it. Perhaps the foreign leader who understood this best was former British Prime Minister Tony Blair. A few months after the invasion of Iraq, during a speech to the US Congress, he addressed Americans who were sceptical of their country's overseas commitments:

> And I know it's hard on America, and in some small corner of this vast country, out in Nevada or Idaho or these places I've never been to, but always wanted to go, I know out there there's a guy getting on with his life, perfectly happily, minding his own business, saying to you, the political leaders of this country, 'Why me? And why us? And why America?'

In retrospect, what is intriguing about Blair's comment is how alienated the people of Idaho and Nevada became from the answers they were given. There is arguably no more Republican state than Idaho. It has consistently been the most pro-Bush state in America, but even in Idaho the president's approval rating dropped below 50 per cent in 2007 (his rating in Nevada fell into negative territory as far back as 2005).

Frustration with Bush's foreign policy has been a key factor in this growing disillusionment. As the 2008 presidential election campaign spread across the American heartland, from Idaho to

Nevada, the extent to which America's battered reputation came up on the hustings was truly remarkable. Apart from the human suffering of war, what rankled most among voters in small towns and suburbs was that the United States was now perceived as a bully.

Ordinary Americans no longer recognise themselves in their country's global image. This is a good sign for those who are hoping for a reinvention of American foreign policy. Another encouraging sign in the election campaign was the occasional similarities between the two main candidates. Obama and McCain clashed about their approach to rogue regimes, but on the general need for more international cooperation, they were broadly at one.

Straight off the blocks, Barack Obama promised a radically different approach to foreign policy, a consistent balance between Frontier and Ritual. 'America cannot meet the threats of this century alone,' he said in his first big foreign policy speech, 'but the world cannot meet them without America. We must neither retreat from the world nor try to bully it into submission – we must lead the world, by deed and example.'

John McCain has disagreed with aspects of George Bush's foreign policy but seems to share some of the president's assumptions about the world. Yet within weeks of securing the Republican nomination, he travelled to Europe to outline a distinct change in style. He spoke about the need to fight global warming, denounced torture and promised a new era of cooperation between the US and its allies. 'When we believe that international action is necessary ... we will try to persuade our friends that we are right,' he said. 'But we, in return, must also be willing to be persuaded by them.' Hawk or no hawk, McCain was no George Bush.

The desire for cooperation that we have heard from Obama and McCain certainly reflects the views of a critical mass, the Millennial generation. Opinion polls show that 18- to 25-year-olds were much more likely to support compromise with America's allies than were their elders. A majority said that the lesson of 9/11 was that the US needed to be more connected to the world, and a similar majority said that human rights was a very important goal of American foreign policy. Millennials are also more likely to have seen the world; 59 per cent of 18- to 24-year-olds have travelled outside the United States (whereas just one in five Americans of all ages made a foreign trip between 1997 and 2002).

Everything we have heard from John McCain, Barack Obama and the Millennials points to reinvention. But it's not that simple. Perhaps more than any other facet of American life, foreign policy is where Americans seem hopelessly adrift.

Even the Millennials are torn by the challenges America faces. For example, there is a surprisingly hawkish tendency among young people. Just before the invasion of Iraq, Millennials were more supportive of the impending war than other age groups, and one poll found that a narrow majority of young Americans favoured unilateral action against Iran.

Those mixed messages reflect a broader confusion among Americans in general. Polls show that they are capable of simultaneously holding two seemingly opposing views. One survey back in 2004 showed majority support for the notion of pre-emptive military action by the US. But in the same poll, voters said they wanted their leaders to listen to their allies rather than go it alone.

The ability to see equal truth in two contradictory positions is what the psychologists call cognitive dissonance, a phrase that aptly describes the age-old duality behind US foreign policy. But the balance between the competing instincts of Frontier and Ritual is not static; there is movement between the two. And for all the concern about America's global reputation, the trend tells us that Americans are retreating to the safety of the homestead. Fifty-two per cent of people surveyed by CBS News in December 2006 thought the United States 'should mind its own business internationally'. At the darkest days of the Vietnam War, just 36 per cent of Americans held the same view.

This trend is not led by some isolationist vanguard. Instead, we are seeing a great cloak of perplexed indifference settle over the American heartland. After years of war and terror, people there have become desensitised to images of chaos and tired of suffering in the world. They have found the best way to overcome the loss of free security is to pretend that it still exists. Americans still feel vulnerable, but they cope with their doubts by retreating behind the walls of their land of plenty.

The public has a willing ally in the American media, which continues to cut back their coverage of world events after a post-9/11 glut. You can't blame them when you see the ratings foreign news gets these days. When CBS News sent their star presenter, Katie Couric, to Iraq to anchor their evening show, the ratings plunged to a historic low.

In days gone by, the American public had a more direct connection to military conflict. Many more families from the heartland were directly involved in those far-off wars. During World War II, more than one in ten Americans served in the US military. In the course of the war in Iraq, it is down to one out of every 100.

The future of the United States is still intertwined with the future of the world – more so in this post-9/11 globalised world – but the American way of life acts increasingly like a shield, protecting its followers from the outside world. In a strangely un-American way, it rewards them for not looking towards the horizon. But it is hard to be 'mankind's last best hope' if you can't see over the walls of that shining city.

—•—

In all the food courts in all the shopping malls in America, there is the same sense of refuge. But in the Arizona boomburb of Glendale, the experience is just that little bit more intense.

Outside, the temperature is somewhere in the region of 40 to 45 degrees celsius. It's been the hottest summer on record in the Valley of the Sun. The brisk walk across the black asphalt surface of the car park is enough to singe your mortal soul. Up ahead are the doors of the Arrowhead shopping mall, catching the light like water on an oasis.

The first gust of air-conditioned relief marks the onset of a Zen-like state of contentment. It will stay with you throughout your visit, like some spectral personal shopper. All around is abundance and movement – but also calm. After all, there is enough stuff for everyone.

But first, the food court and tasty treats from all across the planet: Japanese at Hibachi-san or Chinese at Panda Express or Italian at Sbarro or Mexican at Taco del Mar and Chevy's or all-American at A&W or Cajun at the Bourbon Street Grill.

This is a place to feel worldly without the intimidating presence of foreignness. It is also a place to gather. The food court offers you the chance to linger among your fellow consumer-citizens in a vague approximation of what they used to do once upon a time in market squares. Actually, this not just the Arrowhead shopping mall, it is the Arrowhead Towne Center. That is *Towne* with an 'e', as in Merry *Olde* England.

Two older ladies in tracksuits power-walk by the food court. Moments later, a middle-aged woman passes in the opposite direction at a similar pace. She is wearing running clothes and has a mini-disc player strapped to her arm and a water bottle in her hand. You can't help but notice there is a definite scarcity of obesity around here: a tell-tale mark of affluence.

The troubles of the world are very far away until you get up to leave the food court. Two tables away is an elderly man wearing a baseball cap which says 'World War II Veteran'. A few steps later and you see that a slightly younger, plumper man is wearing a hat with the words 'Vietnam War Veteran'. What are the odds?

Pretty good, actually, if what you are looking for is the remembrance of past wars. But what about the other type of war: the one being fought right now? The White House continues to declare 'We are a nation at war.' But this doesn't feel like a nation at war.

Apparently, there is a Marine Recruiting office somewhere in the mall. That seems strange. How many kids at the mall make the impulsive decision to become a 'jarhead'? Buy a pair of Oakley shades maybe, but not a one-way ticket to Iraq. It just seems unlikely with all this loveliness around.

'What problems … what problems we got?' That's what high school principal Herman Serignese told us that first Friday night at Saguaro. The words bounce off the glass and steel walls of this 'towne' centre and sweep out the door into the endless expanse of the Boomburb Empire.

Empires are weakened by indulgence – but not the United States. George Bush told his fellow Americans to go shopping after 9/11. Go out and cultivate the brands that bewitch the world, revel in the contentment of your local shopping mall, remind yourself how America earned its 'soft power': the ability to influence people without bombing them. Wasn't it FDR, the great internationalist, who once joked that the way to persuade the Soviets of America's superiority was to drop Sears catalogues on them?

All this talk of shopping and war brings a radical comparison to mind: Arrowhead Towne Center and the Titan Missile Base have a lot in common. They both speak of the same desire to shape the world without ever having to leave home. In both places, there is the same desperate need for sanctuary and similar traces of manipulation.

But here's the big difference: things were clearer back then. During the Cold War, the United States had an obvious enemy, a clear mission and a categorical imperative to make friends and keep friends. It had no choice but to maintain a disciplined balance between Ritual and Frontier. There was no room for drift when it took just 58 seconds to initiate the Apocalypse.

Today, that 'war on terror' has lost its focus; its purpose is diluted; the enemy is everywhere and nowhere. Americans would like to make things right, but what they hear from beyond the walls of their shining city is the low-level hum of a hostile crowd. It feels like a good time to retreat to the stucco house in the desert, to work, to live, to be happy, to be American. To forget.

Americans spent a good part of the last decade coping with life on the Frontier; now they are returning to the warm embrace of Ritual. They are drifting towards a state of profound detachment, and so is their nation's foreign policy. There is certainly still room for hope: a new generation is on the rise; a new president is on the way. There is talk of renewal and re-engagement, but for now it is just talk. It will require more than talk to rouse America from its restless slumber among the sunlit homesteads of Idaho and Nevada.

Conclusion:
The Future

10.
Henderson – The City Shines On

Frank Sinatra said that the colour that gave him most peace was the cobalt hue of the eastern sky just before sunrise. He called it 'Five O'Clock Vegas blue'. Sadly, whatever solace there is in the pre-dawn sky over Las Vegas is burned to a cinder by lunchtime.

Viewed from the top of a nearby suburban hill, the city is an untidy clutter of building blocks littering a pristine desert valley. The Vegas Strip is shrouded in a grimy vanilla mist that seems impermeable to everything but the occasional aeroplane taking off or landing at McCarran airport. The sky doesn't turn blue again until it is well clear of the Strip's signature landmark, the Stratosphere Tower.

Here on the hill, there is another city, where the air is clear and the sun shines bright. This is Sin City's wholesome half-brother, Henderson. You have a casual fling with Las Vegas. You marry Henderson.

You can get a decent view of the Vegas Strip from the manicured lawns of Henderson's open-air 'lifestyle center', the District at Green Valley Ranch. The District also offers you a chance to channel the mystical spirit of some long-lost small town. It describes itself as 'a place to meet friends for a cup of coffee, to stroll along a tree-lined main street, to read a book under a tree, or enjoy an afternoon picnic.' The words 'organic', 'vibrant' and 'diverse' leap out from the center's website, as does the mention of the 'vintage-style' carousel with 32 animals ('...even a frog').

One of the great ironies of American life, at this time of reinvention, is that the nostalgia for times past is most intense in places which burn with ambition and drive. Henderson is one such place. The city was created during World War II to supply the magnesium used in munitions and aircraft. When the war ended, the town was literally surplus to requirements. In 1947, the US government offered Henderson for sale.

The town was rescued by a group of local businessmen who saw potential in the hillside community. More than half a century later, Henderson is the second largest city in Nevada and has just emerged from a period of staggering growth. The city is officially a boomburb, and its population is expected to soar to 517,000 by 2030.

Henderson started out making products, but now the city itself is the product. The 'Henderson Lifestyle' pitches itself at the higher end of the market, and offers a selection of premium residential developments laid out across the gently sloping black volcanic earth of the McCullough Mountain range. Their names speak of superior aspirations: Anthem, Black Mountain Vistas, Calico Ridge, Champion Village, Green Valley Ranch, Madeira Canyon, Seven Hills, Tuscany Village.

The city's official slogan is 'Henderson – a Place to Call Home'. The man responsible for keeping the promise is Mayor Jim Gibson, a clean-cut lawyer who speaks in reassuring bass tones. His father was one of the engineers sent to Britain during the war to learn the secrets of processing magnesium, considered by the allies to be a 'miracle metal'. More than a half century later, Jim Gibson presides over a miracle of another kind.

'Back in 1990, Henderson had a population of 64,000,' he says; 'today, we are approaching 280,000 people. The kind of growth we are experiencing is mind-numbing. We open more than one school every month in this county.'

Other Sunbelt cities have had similar growth spurts, but

Henderson has reached a higher stage of suburban evolution. It does not have the same provisional quality of other boom-burbs; it feels complete, even as the building continues. Social innovation is at the heart of its expansion, making Henderson the kind of cosmopolitan brand that cities like Gilbert and Surprise aspire to be.

The Mayor agrees to meet on a pathway which winds around the back of the city's open-air auditorium, the largest in Nevada. It's a scenic spot offering panoramic views of Las Vegas and the upper reaches of Henderson, but it also gives the Mayor a chance to underscore his city's refinement.

In the auditorium the night before, the Moscow Ballet concluded a series of performances of *The Nutcracker*. The Henderson Symphony Orchestra are about to return to its stage to perform Beethoven's Sixth Symphony. The venue will soon celebrate its tenth annual festival of 'Shakespeare in the Park'.

Henderson's pursuit of high culture stems from a ferociously acquisitive instinct, an obsessive desire to stand out. It has the only bird preserve in Nevada, the biggest recreational facility and more park land per capita than any other city in the state. It is rated the sixth-best walking city in America, and in 2006, it was ranked 20th in the CNN/*Money* list of the top 100 places to live in the US.

This is a fine place to put down roots, as long as you share its ambitions. The people who come are a diverse group of American winners. The actor Tony Curtis has a house here, as does Pierre Omidyar, the man who founded eBay. Both Gladys Knight and Brandon Flowers of rock band The Killers have made Henderson their home.

Mayor Jim Gibson still has grand ambition for his city, even after all that mind-numbing growth. Few people talk of a desire to resolve Frontier and Ritual as explicitly as he does. He speaks with evangelical passion about the need to conserve Henderson's desert roots. He wants people to remember that they live on the edge, the meeting point between humanity and wilderness. He speaks with sadness about the growing scarcity of water in the region and the obstacle it poses to his city's onward march.

As he speaks, the Mayor echoes themes from the New Urbanist movement which is beginning to make an impact on the thinking of boomburb planners. He embraces their recipe for 'Smart Growth', which requires pretty basic ingredients: more walking and less driving; neighbourhoods or nothing.

'It's real important to have open space,' the mayor says, gesturing towards the lush, sylvan trail winding away from us, 'to have parks and trail systems. It is something we have to develop in this part of the country. We also try and locate schools, shopping and parks within new developments so that we don't have to bus kids to schools across the valley.'

Jim Gibson has been working with a group of private developers to create Nevada's first large-scale New Urbanist development. The name of the project says it all: Inspirada. When it's complete, Inspirada will be one of the largest communities of its kind in the US, with 26,000 residents, 300 acres of parkland and more than 20 miles of trails for walking and biking.

The development will not have any gated communities; instead, there will be seven individual villages, each with a theme drawn from music, art, athletics, dance, exploration, painting and science. The villages will be built around a central square with schools, police stations and fire stations.

And at the heart of it all will be a town centre like they used to have in the olden days, with shopping, eating and entertainment within a tight network of streets. In choosing a name for this monument to the reinvention of American rituals, they settled on Civita.

This development promises a hybrid architectural style that

reclaims the best of the past. Houses will be built closer to streets and cars will be parked in hidden garages. Open balconies, porches and patios will be returned to suburban life. Gone are the rows and rows of identical stucco mansions. Instead, neighbourhoods will have a mix of apartments, townhouses and family homes, all built with individual character and an array of different materials.

'We fell in love with our cars and fell out of love with our neighbours,' says John Ritter, the leader of the consortium developing Inspirada. 'The street ends up looking like a line of garages.'

New Urbanism aims to rein in the urban sprawl that is dragging America towards the precipice. So, Inspirada will have higher-density housing, and each new resident will be within walking distance of essential amenities. The developers are also planning to build light rail stations so that if Henderson develops a mass transit system in the future, Inspirada will be the first community to be connected.

Inspirada offers to save the boomburb experiment from its own contradictions. On paper, it's hard to find a flaw in the logic, but there are critics who say Smart Growth ignores the needs of hard-working families fleeing the chaos of the cities.

'I view New Urbanism and Smart Growth as an assault on my quality of life,' writes Steve Greenhut, a columnist for the *Orange County Register*; 'as an attempt to take away my square footage and my yard. In their world, a guy on a newspaper salary would not be able to live in a nice house with four bedrooms surrounded by open space. Only the wealthy elite would get to live like that.'

This is a common refrain, that the New Urbanists are a bunch of wealthy liberals who want to retreat into a cosmopolitan dream world. Here's how David Brooks in *On Paradise Drive* sums up the style-obsessed residents of New Urbanist zones:

They want sidewalks, stores with overpriced French children's clothes to browse in after dinner, six-dollar-a-cone ice cream vendors, and plenty of restaurants. They don't want suburban formula restaurants. They want places where they can offer disquisitions on the reliability of the risotto, where the predinner complimentary bread slices look like they were baked by Burgundian monks, and where they can top off their dinner with a self-righteous carrot smoothie.

Oh, the horror.

Every left-leaning movement in American life will eventually be cast as an elitist assault on decent middle-class people, an attempt to impose alien values. It is a charge the New Urbanists are struggling to overcome. They say Smart Growth will remove the walls between the haves and have-nots. The Congress for the New Urbanism says it 'promotes the end of segregation between rich and poor. ...We support the inclusion of a variety of housing in every development — allowing apartments to mix with houses, and rentals to mix with owner-occupied housing'.

As an environmental movement, New Urbanism seems to be winning the argument, but as a force for social change, it is on shakier ground. In the wrong hands, this new ethical vision of suburbia could encourage the fragmentation of American life rather than prevent it. Smart Growth could be used as a convenient label for those who want to retreat behind the walls of secure enclaves populated by like-minded neighbours (presumably to stir their risotto and sip contentedly on carrot smoothies).

Henderson has embraced New Urbanism as a logical extension of its prized autonomy. Henderson worked hard to break free of the gravitational pull of the other cities in the Las Vegas area, and is determined to remain fixed in its own unique orbit.

'We don't rely on them for resources of any kind,' says Mayor

Jim Gibson, 'and we surely don't have any dependence on their decisions. It's all our decisions. It's all about trying to do it the way we do it in Henderson, the Henderson way, the fiercely independent way.'

The city requires an equal passion for self-reliance from those who come to build in Henderson. Each new development is required to have its own homeowners' association, which may offer a uniquely neighbourly form of self-rule but also tends to privatise civic action. The associations also require residents to sign up to 'civic covenants, conditions and restrictions' which can often create a strictly controlled form of public life in boomburn developments (some experts say that New Urbanist developments often have the toughest regulations). Officially, these communities are known as 'common interest developments', but the sceptics have another name for them: 'privatopias'.

The rise of the privatopia mirrors the growth of the boomburb; there were 10,000 homeowners' associations back in 1970 and the number had grown to 260,000 by 2004. One study found that four out of five houses built in America since the 1990s are in developments controlled by homeowners' associations.

Privatopias may seem like a recent invention, but home-owners' associations are just another expression of that eternal American search for sanctuary in a society of perpetual change. You could even argue that the notion of privatopia was alive and well in John Winthrop's day. Those early Puritan settlements in Plymouth, Massachusetts, and Jamestown, Virginia, look very much like early models of common-interest communities.

In *People of Paradox*, historian Michael Kammen argues the early settlers quickly acquired a tribal state of mind as a way of coping with the jumble of identities they saw around them. 'In becoming so exclusive and withdrawn,' Kammen writes, 'they were demonstrating one kind of defense mechanism against an unexpectedly plural society.'

This has a familiar ring to it, and that same impulse may have played a part in the initial rush to suburbia. The critics have always claimed that suburbanites moved out of the big cities to escape their increasing racial diversity. In Henderson, they may have a point; almost 80 per cent of the people who live in the city are white, and just 10 per cent are Hispanic, well below the Nevada state average.

Henderson tells us one thing about the instincts of the new American suburb, but other boomburbs tell us something completely different. Just across the valley, the boomburb of North Las Vegas is a model of racial integration. Thirty-seven per cent of its residents are Hispanic, thirty-seven per cent are white, and one in five is African-American. All told, one quarter of the people who live in North Las Vegas are foreign-born. It would not be America if they did not have a nice, neat label to describe such a place: 'cosmoburb'.

The contrast between North Las Vegas and Henderson is a warning to those who would apply sweeping generalisations to the boomburbs. Remember, these cities organise themselves as distinct brands offering tailored lifestyles to competing groups in a restless society. The nature of the modern American suburb is that the 'Henderson way' will be different to the 'North Las Vegas way' or the 'Surprise way'. However, there is something that these vast new urban communities have in common, and that is a profound shift from Frontier to Ritual.

Consider Henderson as the latest incarnation of the 'city on the hill'. Its fierce independence and missionary zeal prove that the spirit of the Frontier is still working its dark magic in the new Wild West. But Henderson's particular success is in its resurrection of Ritual. The city offers high ground just as a rising tide of uncertainty and division threatens America; it provides sanctuary from the problems of an increasingly hostile world. After years of conflict and division, Henderson promises the comfort of home.

The reinvention of America is essentially the renewal of the concept of community. It began when the pioneers of the desert suburbs became settlers and set out to soften the hard edge of the Sunbelt Frontier. It may have started as a shallow nostalgia for small-town life, but it became a quest for civil society. Decades of political polarisation and uncontrolled suburban expansion have eroded the common ground in American life. The evolving civic traditions of the boomburb are part of the effort to restore it.

The clash of Frontier and Ritual in the Sunbelt provided a spark for reinvention, but it would not have caught fire without the explosive collision of transformational forces. The power of social technology, the historic surge in immigration and the rise of a civic generation have invested this American reinvention with unstoppable power.

The speed and direction of that reinvention are still up for grabs. In its most positive form it will follow the lead of people with vision, from Freestyle Evangelicals to the New Urbanists. At its best, it will embrace the opportunities of a more connected world and confront the challenge of an increasingly fragile environment.

However, Ritual also has a dark side, and Henderson shows us the power of that counter-current in the reinvention of America. Just as hope brings the promise of progress, fear and indifference have prompted a retreat from the world. Many Americans are seeking sanctuary behind the increasingly imposing wall of their own private shining cities. The boomburbs offer them the opportunity to lives as individuals within a very narrow collective: people just like them.

Henderson is a battlefield for the competing instincts of this American reinvention. It embraces change and offers a retreat from it. It is imbued with a vision of the American dream that is simultaneously dynamic and static. Before we leave the 'city on the hill', it is worth hearing Mayor Jim Gibson's views on the pursuit of happiness, the Henderson way.

We're trying to establish it here. Then, rather than
going out to market it, we want it to be ready, so
that when you're ready, we're ready. And this is the
place where the American dream really comes full
circle. That's how we see it.

The Mayor is a genuine visionary. But he makes one mistake.
He talks of the American dream as if it was a destination. It's
not. It's an everlasting journey with countless different stops.

—•—

When you make hard and fast predictions about the United
States, they have a habit of coming back to haunt you. But it
would be wrong to leave the reinvention of America hanging
midway between hope and doubt.

The first imponderable is the future of the American
economy. Logic suggests that a major recession would bring the
last twenty years of movement to an end. If migration dried up,
then the Great Dispersal would be over and so would what Jim
Gibson called the 'mind-numbing' growth of the Sunbelt
boomburbs. Without the kinetic power of those rapidly expanding communities, the reinvention of America would struggle to
maintain its current breathless pace.

Long-term forecasts look good for those evolving desert
communities. Two real estate professors at Wharton College in
Pennsylvania published a study of property trends across the
United States and concluded that the Southwest will continue
to grow strongly. 'Prospective real estate developers,' they
advised, 'had better buy a good pair of sunglasses and some
sunblock.'

The survey predicts that Clark County, which contains Las
Vegas, will have grown by a little over 80 per cent between 2000
and 2020, adding almost a million new residents. Other states in

the Sunbelt continue to lure millions their way. The Wharton professors predict that eight out of the top ten fastest-growing counties in America between 2000 and 2020 will be in the Southwest and California.

The survey says that the fundamental strength of Sunbelt states is that they have mastered 'a new paradigm of growth'. Migrants are no longer attracted to cities because of plentiful jobs and houses; they are looking for a better quality of life where 'highly skilled workers, consumers, will want to spend their time and money.' They are also attracted by sunshine: 'In short, people are moving to "the bright side".'

The Sunbelt can also expect to benefit from that continuing surge in immigration. New arrivals in America tend to converge on areas where previous generations of immigrants settled. In the case of Latino and Hispanic immigrants, the first destination of choice will continue to be the Sunbelt.

The problem with the Wharton study is that it was published in 2006, before the sub-prime crisis hit. The fundamental strengths it highlighted have not changed, but its forecasts will have to be revised, particularly in light of census figures released in 2008. They showed that the Sunbelt cities continue to expand, but at a slower rate than before. For example, Phoenix and its surrounding county grew by a little over 100,000 people between 2006 and 2007. One hundred and thirty thousand people moved there the previous year.

The slowdown will be sharpest where the property market is in the most trouble. Some demographers, like Kenneth Johnson of the University of New Hampshire, say that the census figures reflect only 'the front edge' of the housing crisis, and that Sunbelt growth will slow significantly. William Frey of the Brookings Institution prefers to use the phrase 'migration correction' to describe the immediate future.

Another potential challenge to Sunbelt life is the relentless rise in fuel prices. Official statistics showed the petrol bill of the average suburban family more than doubled between 2003 and 2008, and the rising cost of driving has already reduced the value of property in distant suburbs of big American cities.

Perhaps this price shock is exactly what the Sunbelt Boomburbs need: another incentive for reinvention. If these desert communities are to remain an engine of transformation, they are going to need a lot less gas-guzzling sprawl and lot more of the sustainable appeal of New Urbanism.

Make no mistake, the forces behind this reinvention are unstoppable, even if they face a stiffer oncoming wind in the the years ahead. If you have trouble accepting that prediction, then take a little trip into the future.

Imagine it is the year 2050.

About 430 million people now live in America (up from 296 million in 2005). If you are white, you are now officially a minority. One out of every five people passing you on the street was born in another country (double the number in 2005). Close to one in three of those faces is Hispanic (double the number in 2005). One in ten is Asian-American, and 27 million Americans are a combination of two or more races.

You will notice that a lot more people are over 65, about twice as many. In fact, the first-born Millennials are reaching retirement. They have had a good run, after controlling American politics for close on four decades. There may be many more older people, but immigration has kept America young in comparison with the rest of the western world. Back in Europe, the median age has climbed to over fifty. Here in America, it is still below forty, and one in four people on that average street are teenagers.

Something certainly did happen in America, but it had very little to do with the outcome of the 2008 presidential election.

—•—

The most dangerous form of predictions are forecasts of the American political climate, but let me lay out a few scenarios for the politics of reinvention.

The first is the worst-case scenario. We have just found out that there are two rapidly expanding groups within the US population: young immigrant workers and older, white retirees. That raises the prospect of a growing schism in American society based on race and generation.

You can already detect the first signs of generational tension. In a survey by the Pew Research Center, 50 per cent of voters said that they would be less likely to vote for a candidate who was over 70 (fewer people have second thoughts about a gay or Muslim candidate). Clearly, this poses a challenge for John McCain, who, if elected president, would be 72 when taking office. McCain copes with the age issue with his trademark wisecracks; 'I am older than dirt and have more scars than Frankenstein,' he likes to joke. There is an edge to the humour.

Concerns over McCain's age point to generational cracks, but Barack Obama's campaign sits right on top of a fault line. His greatest source of strength is his overwhelming support among young people. Exit polls taken during the primary season show that he won the backing of 60 per cent of voters under 30.

Meanwhile, his greatest failure is his inability to strike a chord with older voters; 57 per cent of voters 65 and over went with Hillary Clinton in the primaries. Particularly striking were the results in key battleground states like Ohio, where just one in four voters who were white and over sixty supported Obama.

What we are seeing is a rivalry between competing life experiences. Millennial voters have known nothing but high immigration, good times and rapid technological change. Older voters have lived through war, recession and social upheaval. One generation seeks change and another craves security. 'So the older generation may be convinced of the younger generation's naïveté,' writes columnist Ellen Goodman, 'the younger may complain of their elders' time warp.'

The generations also have completely different experiences of racial identity. Four out of ten Millennials are minorities, compared with two out of ten senior citizens. To put it bluntly, young Americans are the most racially diverse generation alive, while the oldest Americans are the whitest.

Millions of young and diverse Americans are drawn to the Sunbelt, leaving the Northern and Midwestern states with slower-growing, aging white populations. Many older, white Americans live in the Rustbelt, which has suffered sharp economic decline in recent decades, so that racial-generational divide is sharpened by geography and economics. States like Ohio, Michigan and Pennsylvania scream out with the doubts and frustrations of older, white Americans at a time of traumatic change.

America's most insightful demographer, William Frey, has written a fascinating paper on the demographic dimension of the 2008 election, in which he focuses on the importance of these older, greyer battleground states:

> In these states, voter profiles and issues differ strikingly from those in states with larger minority populations. And the fact that whites tend to be more well represented in the voting population than any other minority group gives them an outsized influence, relative to their population, in most states' electorates.

Barack Obama is beatable in those Rustbelt states which have the power to decide elections. Any combination of Ohio, Pennsylvania, Michigan and Florida (which has such a high proportion of over-65s) could well prevent him becoming the first president of the American reinvention. If this happens, it will happen because many people in these states know the pain of transformation, and see an empty, threatening tone in what Obama says.

In one sense, the contest between John McCain and Barack Obama is just another battle between Frontier and Ritual, with Obama representing that instinctual attraction to change and McCain standing for order and security. But in the worst-case scenario, it could also be the first battle of a racial and generational conflict. Here's how William Frey put it (even before Obama and McCain officially became nominees):

> It might be said that a possible presidential match up between white, pre-Baby Boomer John McCain and post-ethnic, post-Baby Boomer Barack Obama represent bookends to the transformation America's electorate is going through. The problem for these candidates, and others in the near term, is that they will have to deal with a country that is still balkanized, with states and regions changing in different ways and at different speeds, as part of the continued transformation of our racial demography.

This racial-generational split is a wild card in the 2008 election. It also brings an unpredictable quality to the reinvention of America. Generational tension may ease as the Millennials begin to grow old themselves; race may become less divisive in a future where every American is a minority. But for now, in our worst-case scenario, the reinvention of America will be a tense, faltering process, even if its outcome is preordained.

There is a more hopeful scenario, and once again, the Sunbelt is the agent of change. The sprawling Sunbelt cities may be warming the Earth, but they are also emerging as a political thermostat for America. The people who live in the boomburbs are optimistic and positive, and they retreat from extremism. They are drawing politics back to the middle ground. They want politicians to talk about quality-of-life issues like job growth, climate and water, and not wedge issues like gay marriage and abortion. They are bucking the dysfunctional trends that have crippled American political life for the past three decades.

Other parts of the United States have become more polarised in recent years. There has been a dramatic rise in the number of 'landslide counties', where Republicans or Democrats have won by margins of over 20 per cent. Things are different in the boomburbs, where the overwhelming trend is away from polarisation. As we have already seen, most of the counties containing boomburbs are considered swing counties. Henderson is a good example: John Kerry won there in 2004 with just a 52 per cent majority.

As their cities settle and they forge deeper civic bonds, tribal loyalties seem to matter less. Boomburb voters are no longer a partisan base, ready to be fired up by outrage and anger. They are looking for practical solutions and common ground. If it were up to voters in the Sunbelt to set the national agenda, the era of hyper-polarised politics would end tomorrow. The good news is that Sunbelt voters are increasingly setting the agenda. As boomburbs have expanded, their political influence has increased exponentially. They are transforming Sunbelt states like New Mexico, Nevada and Arizona into swing states, dramatically increasingly their influence at election time. More and more, the boomburbs' moderating instincts are setting the tone of politics in this age of reinvention.

The fastest-growing suburbs in the Sunbelt still lean towards the Republicans, but Democrats are hoping that, as they continue to evolve, the boomburbs will deliver a political realignment. In their dreams, that realignment begins in 2008.

Remember, it was Sunbelt conservatives who led the Republicans to four decades of domination. Now it is young people and immigrants in the Sunbelt who are the most potent force for change in America. In California, for example, 56 per cent of eligible voters under the age of 30 are minorities; in Texas, the figure is 51 per cent. Polls suggest that more young people and more immigrants equals more votes for the Democrats.

The race for the White House may ultimately be decided by white retirees voting in Ohio, but it could also hinge on the turnout of young Latinos in New Mexico. But in the short term, the evolving political culture of the Sunbelt is yet another wild card, just like that racial-generational divide.

In 2008, the Republicans have given themselves the best possible chance in the Sunbelt by choosing an Arizona senator who reflects the post-partisan sensibilities of the boomburbs. That was a smart move at a time when the prevailing winds favour the Democrats. 'No disrespect to the other candidates,' said Republican pollster Glen Bolger, 'but if anyone else had been nominated we'd be toast.'

Republicans can also draw comfort from Barack Obama's poor performance in the Sunbelt during his primary battle against Hillary Clinton. He lost in all the key western battlegrounds: California, Nevada, Arizona, Texas and New Mexico. His appeal for change was blunted by rising economic insecurity, and he ran poorly among Latinos. Obama will have to rectify his problems in the Sunbelt if he is to win his contest against McCain.

It is too early to speak definitively about a realignment in US politics, but the evolution of the Sunbelt is already having a positive influence. The civic preferences of boomburbs are pushing politics back onto common ground, moderating the tone of debate and taking the hard edge off of ideological conflict. It is hard to overestimate just how important such a post-partisan trend is to the reinvention of America. Three decades of culture war have paralysed the political process in the United States. 'A can-do country is now saddled with a do-nothing political process,' says *Newsweek's* Fareed Zakaria, 'designed for partisan battle rather than problem solving.'

The 2008 presidential election is a first step in renewing the health of the US political system, no matter who wins. You may not believe Barack Obama and John McCain when they talk of an end to an era of partisanship, but neither candidate would have got this far if there were not a genuine appetite in America for a new style of politics.

Think of this campaign as a defeat for the Woody Hayes School of Politics. Hayes was a revered coach in American college football who made famous a style of play called 'three yards and a cloud of dust'. It was a full-frontal assault on your enemy in which winning was the only thing.

The Woody Hayes School of Politics has a long list of famous graduates, from Richard Nixon and his winning strategy of 'positive polarisation', to Bush's political guru Karl Rove, who believed that the key to victory was firing up a party's ideological base. This school of politics teaches it students to played hard for control of the margins; there is nothing to be gained by consensus.

In the Woody Hayes School, the greatest personal virtue is never giving up. In her darkest hour, Hillary Clinton would invoke that credo, as she met the hard-pressed folks of the Rustbelt, signing autographs on boxing gloves, invoking the name of Rocky Bilboa. 'We need a president who's a fighter again,' she told a rally in Indiana, in the twilight of her presidential campaign. 'Getting knocked down and getting back up: that's the story of America, right?'

It is just one American story – a frontier tale, the myth of the rugged individual in a lonely battle against the world. But it is not the story of America's reinvention. Three yards and a cloud of dust no longer cuts it with a Millennial generation reared on connectivity and consensus, or voters in the boomburbs sick of partisan combat. As an advancing tide of change sweeps across their nation, a steady surge of Americans are moving to higher ground.

For some Americans, reinvention also means retreat. On that higher ground, they seek refuge in their own shining cities, behind increasingly imposing walls, where the problems of the world seem very far away.

The United States is entering an era of change, no matter who wins the race for the White House in 2008. That reinvention will be dramatic and potentially traumatic.

What is happening to America is so much bigger than any one politician, any one election. What is happening in America right now is so much more important than America.

—•—

In March 2008, a delegation from China travelled to the small but perfectly-formed Arizona suburb of Buckeye. Not yet a boomburb, it was the second fastest-growing municipality in the United States in 2007, and is well known in planning circles as home to the New Urbanist development of Verrado.

The Chinese travelled to the Sonoran desert to examine the lessons of the Great Dispersal. The most dynamic nation on earth had come to learn from the fastest-growing region of America. The reinvention of America had officially become a global phenomenon.

The tipping point had come earlier. In 2005, the *San Francisco Chronicle* wrote about Napa Valley, not the mecca of American wine-making, but a new development 30 miles outside Beijing, where the planners attempted a very familiar fusion of Californian and Mediterranean. 'Rustic stone is widely used,' said the sales brochure, 'with rich stucco colors, along with wood shutters and wrought-iron accents, to create an intimate scale and village-like feel,' The architects who designed Napa Valley are from Orange County.

Every year, the world puts an extra 60 million people in its urban areas. The boomburbs have become a living laboratory of what to do, and what not to do, when faced with a booming population and unstoppable aspirations for the good life. From Lahore to Buenos Aires, planners are learning the lessons of the Sunbelt, for better or for worse.

Isn't that just like the Americans, to imagine their bad habits are innovations which must be forced on the rest of the world?

It feels better when you put it like that, doesn't it? It is so much easier to cope with Americans if you remain sceptical and detached.

But detachment comes at a price. It blinds us to a stark reality: there is no such thing as an American bad habit. There is no such thing as an American innovation for that matter. The United States is a great, big laboratory for the very worst and the very best of the human spirit. 'American' is just another word for the stuff that happens there first.

Think of about it like that, and you will find it easier to cope when you suddenly realise that this American reinvention has become part of your life.

You may have already realised it. There must have been a point in the pages of this book when you said to yourself, 'I recognise this'. The similarities must have jumped out at you when you read about YouTube, MySpace and the dizzying promise of the digital age. That is not exclusively American; by definition, it could never be.

Nor are the Millennials a uniquely American generation. They are among us. They may be you. A generation that has known nothing but success, diversity and the connected spirit of a digital age. This is America, but it could be Ireland.

Consider a nation that is being transformed by immigration, buffeted by economic uncertainty and bogged down by urban sprawl. It is America, but it could be Ireland.

Think of reinvention. It is America, but it could be Ireland.

Bibliographical Note

The central themes of this book emerged while I was researching and writing the documentary series *American Dream: Dead or Alive*, broadcast on RTÉ in February 2008. The series was directed by Ruan Megan, produced by Adrian Lynch of Animo productions and filmed by Colm Whelan. I am very grateful to them for supplying me with DVD copies of original interviews and footage filmed during our travels in the Sunbelt in the autumn and winter of 2007 (particular thanks to Colm for his photographs). The detailed accounts of my conversations and encounters in Saguaro High School, Orangewood Elementary, Radiant Church, on the US–Mexican border, and other locations in Surprise, Gilbert, Henderson, Phoenix and Las Vegas, are largely drawn from the video record of that journey.

For the historical background to Radiant Church I relied on a *New York Times* article written by Jonathan Mahler in March 2005. I learned about the background to the creation of Ladera Ranch from an April 2006 article in the *Washington Post* written by Stephanie McCrummen. A series of articles in the *Las Vegas Review Journal* provided information about the development of the Inspirada development in Henderson.

The details of my encounters with the Lucio Family in Brownsville, the Coffmans in Fullerton, and all other scenes in Orange County, Los Angeles and Texas, are drawn from my personal notes and video footage filmed by RTÉ cameramen Nick Dolan and Cedric Culliton, during coverage of the 2008 presidential primaries. I relied on personal notes and photographs to help me write the account of my visit to the Titan Missile Base in spring 2008.

In setting out to examine the life of the new American suburb, I have been inspired by the work of *New York Times* columnist and author David Brooks, in particular by his book *On Paradise Drive*. By far the most informed observer of the Boomburb phenomenon is Professor Robert E. Lang, the founder of the Metropolitan Institute at Virginia Tech. With Jennifer LeFurgy, he wrote *Boomburbs*, which is an essential reference book for anyone seeking to chart America's future (LeFurgy's 2005 paper for the Metropolitan Institute on voting patterns in the boomburbs was also an important source in this book).

In trying to understand the history of the suburb I found Kenneth Jackson's *Crabgrass Frontier* to be an invaluable guide. J. Eric Oliver provides a critical assessment of politics in the suburbs in *Democracy in Suburbia*, while New Urbanist planners Andres Duany, Elizabeth Plater-Zyberk and Jeff Speck deliver a fascinating and challenging critique of past failures in their book, *Suburban Nation*.

Several authors guided me as I tried to frame those central themes of Frontier and Ritual. I was particularly impressed by historian Michael Kammen's stylish classic, *People of Paradox*. My favourite books on the history of the American West are *Frontiers*, by Robert V. Hine and John Mack Faragher, and *The Fabric of America*, by Andro Linklater. Myles Dungan has skillfully recorded the Irish role on the American frontier in *How the Irish Won the West*. The essential guide to the history of American conservativism is *The Right Nation*, by John Micklethwait and Adrian Wooldridge. Anatol Lieven provides an edgy, provocative history of American nationalism and the Jacksonian tradition in *America Right or Wrong*.

It is impossible to gauge American attitudes to the rest of the world by listening to US politicians. Instead, buy a copy of *America Against the World* by Andrew Kohut and Bruce Stokes. It is a distillation of some of the most important surveys of US and world opinion conducted by the Pew Research Centers and has been an essential reference for this book. For anyone who is still confounded by the world-view of the Bush administration I highly recommend *The One Per Cent Doctrine*, by Ron Suskind.

In trying to assess the role of the imperial instinct in American history, I have turned to Niall Ferguson and his book *Collossus*, Josef Joffe's *Uberpower* and *Are We Rome?* by Cullen Murphy. For a partial but provocative view of the immigration debate in the United States it is well worth reading Samuel Huntington's *Who Are We?* To illustrate the long-term benefits of immigration for the United States, I relied heavily on the work of Fareed Zakaria, in particular his essay *The Future of American Power*, published in the May/June 2008 edition of *Foreign Affairs*.

Robert Frank illustrates the growing economic disparities in America in a very colourful way in *Richistan*. For a deeper understanding of the future of the American dream, it is worth following the ongoing research of the Economic Mobility Project at the Brookings Institution in Washington, particularly its February 2008 report, which informed my thinking on social mobility.

In order to put the 2008 presidential election in context, I dipped into some of the best political biographies and memoirs of recent years. Barack Obama's second book, *The Audacity of Hope*, is helpful enough, but the first, *Dreams from My Father*, is far superior in explaining what makes this man tick. To understand the depth of John McCain's appeal, it is well worth reading the book he wrote with his long-time adviser Mark Salter, *Faith of My Fathers*. For a better understanding of the mixture of hope and doubt which characterised the Clinton dynasty, I would recommend *A Woman in Charge* by Carl Bernstein and *My Life* by Bill Clinton.

The best commentary on the rise of the Millennial Generation is *Millenials Rising*, written by Neil Howe and William Strauss. Morley Winograd and Michael D. Hais have written an important book about the political potential of this generation in *Millennial*

Makeover, as has Michael Connery in *Youth to Power*. For a hugely entertaining and critical take on the Millennials, I highly recommend *X Saves the World* by Jeff Gordiner. Among the reports I consulted while researching the Millennials were *The Progressive Generation*, published by the Center for American Progress in May 2008, and a survey of Youth Voter Turnout, compiled by Rock The Vote during the 2008 presidential primary season.

Any book about change in American society must contain some reference to the work of William H. Frey of the Brookings Institution and the University of Michigan. He is by far the most important demographer in the United States and during my research I kept coming back to his record of the dramatic evolution of American society, in particular his paper on *Race, Immigration and America's Changing Electorate*, published by Brookings in February 2008, and his report *The Racial Generation Gap*, published by the Milken Institute in 2007.

One of the most rewarding discoveries of my research was a book about the history of the all-American corporation, U-Haul, called *A Noble Function* by Luke Krueger. I was also happy to return to the pages of *The Long Tail* by Chris Anderson, which remains one of the most important books of the Internet age. It was also a joy to dip back into two all-time favourites, *The Great Gatsby* by F. Scott Fitzgerald and *American Pastoral* by Phillip Roth.

Finally, this book is a product of its age and relied heavily on the research tools of the Internet. I would have been lost without the city-data website, which provided information on everything from political affiliations in US cities and towns to their racial composition. Zillow.com provided detail on property values in the communities featured in this book and Meetup.com was an entertaining guide to their hidden social life. The Census bureau was an essential source in almost every chapter. RealClearPolitics and Politico provided an invaluable running commentary on the 2008 presidential election, and a surprisingly diverse range of other subjects. As for Wikipedia and YouTube ... words can't express my gratitude.

Index